A practical guide to searching LGBTQIA historical records

I0129092

This book provides a number of effective tools to aid in the recovery of LGBTQIA+ historic material, including extensive glossary and non-glossary written descriptions as well as guidance for using terms and phrases to search effectively online and offline.

Researching hidden and forbidden people from the past can be extremely difficult. Terminology used to write about LGBTQIA+ people shifts over time. Legal terminology enforces certain set terms, which some writers use but others reject to avoid informing or disgusting a reading public. Often written descriptions contain no set terminology at all. How then can LGBTQIA+ people be found in historic records? This book provides practical tools for researchers who want to uncover materials from online or hard-copy sources, including: keyword(s) covering various sexual orientations and gender diversity, along with how and when to use them; tips for effectively searching in online newspaper archives; information about how to use genealogy, auction and social media sites to uncover information; suggestions about searching in online and physical libraries; advice on researching in physical archives and the types of collections which can yield results; and guidance about researching in museums that collect and display LGBTQIA+ content.

This guide is a short, straightforward, jargon-free and accessible companion for doing historical research on lesbian, gay, bisexual, transgender, queer, intersex, asexual and other non-normative research subjects. It is a useful resource for students and scholars alike in archive studies, history or gender and sexuality studies.

Norena Shopland has a master's degree in heritage studies. Originally from Cardiff, she has worked for the British Museum, National Museums Scotland, the Museum of London and other heritage organisations. Now specialising in LGBTQIA+ studies, women's histories and Welsh history, she is responsible for several ground-breaking projects. Norena conceived and secured a National Heritage Lottery Fund (NHLF) grant for Welsh Pride, the first project in Wales to highlight the country's LGBTQIA+ people, allies and events. She managed Gender Fluidity, the first funded transgender project in Wales. Her book *Forbidden Lives: LGBT Stories from Wales* is the first completely historical work on Welsh sexual orientation and gender identity. Norena lectures extensively and has appeared in the press, radio and TV. Her current projects include working with the Big Pit National Coal Museum on the first exhibition on women miners in Wales, working with Swansea's Waterfront Museum on an exhibition of Welsh button badges and supporting Race Council Cymru on their Windrush Cymru NHLF project. Her books include *The Curious Case of the Eisteddfod Baton*, which celebrates Welsh choral singing and the mining of Welsh gold; *The Veronal Mystery*, which examines a real-life gay crime, and *Women in Male Attire: Their Fight to Wear Trousers*, which is forthcoming from Pen and Sword Books in June 2021.

LGBTQ Histories

Queers in State Socialism
Cruising 1970s Poland
Edited by Tomasz Basiuk and Jędrzej Burszta

A Practical Guide to Searching LGBTQIA Historical Records
Norena Shopland

https://www.routledge.com/LGBTQ-Histories/book-series/LGBTQH

A practical guide to searching LGBTQIA historical records

Norena Shopland

Routledge
Taylor & Francis Group

LONDON AND NEW YORK

First published 2021
by Routledge
2 Park Square, Milton Park, Abingdon, Oxon OX14 4RN

and by Routledge
605 Third Avenue, New York, NY 10017

First issued in paperback 2022

Routledge is an imprint of the Taylor & Francis Group, an informa business

Publisher's Note
The publisher has gone to great lengths to ensure the quality of this reprint but points out that some imperfections in the original copies may be apparent.

British Library Cataloguing in Publication Data
A catalogue record for this book is available from the British Library

Library of Congress Cataloging-in-Publication Data
A catalog record has been requested for this book

ISBN 13: 978-0-367-56458-2 (pbk)
ISBN 13: 978-0-367-43960-6 (hbk)
ISBN 13: 978-1-003-00678-7 (ebk)

DOI: 10.4324/9781003006787

Typeset in Times New Roman
by Taylor & Francis Books

Contents

Figures

Acknowledgements

Many thanks to my wife Julie Carpenter; my parents Pam and Bob Shopland; Susan Edwards, former archivist at Glamorgan Archives; Rhian Diggins of Glamorgan Archives; John Vincent; Thea Sibbel of IHLIA LGBT Heritage; and Anthony Rhys.

Introduction

In 2017 I wrote *Forbidden Lives: LGBT Stories from Wales* – the first fully historical work looking at the history of sexual orientation and gender diversity in Wales (Shopland 2017). One of my main objectives when writing the book was to include information that either had not been covered widely or had not been published outside of original sources.

The difficulty of locating forbidden or hidden lives in the past quickly became apparent. At first I used existing and plentiful glossaries and guides but quickly found that they contained mostly modern terms, which were of little use for researching subjects prior to the late nineteenth century. In addition, glossaries rarely include timelines or caveats about use. They overlook the creativity of writers as well as the fact that they were required to avoid certain words in settings such as newspapers. During periods when homosexuality was unacceptable, journalists and writers would often craft stories in their own way and ignore standard references to avoid shocking audiences or hinting any encouragement to 'try it at home'.

The shifting nature of sexual orientation and gender diversity terminology makes it important for researchers to understand when and how terms or phrases were used. When modern terms are used to describe LGBTQIA+ people from the past, it places in the reader's mind an image loaded with modern connotations. The word 'homosexual' conjures up an identity, 'a personage' – as philosopher Michel Foucault put it – someone with 'a past, a case history, and a childhood' (Foucault 1980, pp. 42–4). However, for most of history there was no homosexual person, just a physical act of sex. Therefore, when writing of historic LGBTQIA+ people, we use a definition which simply did not exist in their lifetimes. Similarly, we cannot shortcut the varying definitions of the word 'homosexual' by lumping all under one modern term.

Some LGBTQIA+ research guides have been published, but they have the same shortcoming found in many glossaries – most depend on modern terminology. Probably the most comprehensive is *Queering Glamorgan*, a publication by Dr. Daryl Leeworthy and myself (Shopland & Leeworthy 2018). This guide was funded by the Welsh Government and published by Glamorgan Archives. While the title reflects the funding criteria, it can be used with any English-language historical records. In the year after the guide's publication, it was accessed nearly 1,500 times, a remarkable figure for a research guide, which illustrates the need for this type of information.

In *Queering Glamorgan*, I adapted the research methodology I had devised for *Forbidden Lives* to produce the glossary section. This methodology was driven in part by a determination to uncover more women, transgender and intersex people, who are less visible in the historical record. To achieve this, it was helpful to consider not who or what people were but what they were doing. For example, a study of cross-dressing and cross-living yielded a number of stories about individuals we would today regard as lesbian, transgender or intersex. In fact, so successful was the methodology that I recovered over 3,000 stories, of which approximately 80 percent had never appeared outside of their original sources. One outcome of these findings is my forthcoming book *Women in Male Attire: Their Fight to Wear Trousers*, which will be published by Pen and Sword Books in 2021. It challenges the standard historical narrative by demonstrating that thousands of women cross-dressed and cross-lived in order to circumnavigate restrictions on their lives.

Queering Glamorgan acknowledges that not everyone writes in 'glossary speak', so a more comprehensive 'pick-and-mix' type of wordlist is presented that encourages researchers to try out numerous combinations of words and phrases, all taken from original sources.

This book greatly expands the work started in *Queering Glamorgan* and adds new terms, phrases and advice on how to use keyword(s) searches in online and offline sources. While the *Queering Glamorgan* 'pick-and-mix' wordlist is not included here, readers may want to use it in tandem with this guide (Shopland & Leeworthy 2018).

This book is divided roughly into four parts. The first part focuses on terminology. A range of acronyms have emerged from the original LGBT acronym, which has seen Q, I, A and others added. Throughout this book the keyword 'LGBTQIA+' is used to encompass a wide diversity while avoiding any errors of omission. Chapter 1 examines words and phrases considered to be standard reference terms for particular periods. The following three chapters look at more fluid terminology that rarely appears in reference works. The terms are divided into subject areas: lesbian, gay, bisexual, other sexualities and gender diversity.

The second part of the book provides advice for researching in some of the extensive newspaper archives available online. Practical examples using terminology outlined in the previous chapters will show how these types of searches can successfully recover new information.

The third section considers how genealogy and auction sites can provide some interesting results when researching LGBTQIA+ history.

The final part of the book considers both hard copy and online resources in libraries, archives and museums.

The main theme of the book is to provide tools to facilitate research on sexual orientation and gender diversity. Therefore, neither interpretations of words and phrases nor an analysis of the queer past are included as they are outside the scope of this book. For more on these subjects, readers may want to consult works by Jeffrey Weeks (2000), Laura Doan (2013), Matt Cook (2003) and the *Palgrave Advances in the Modern History of Sexuality* (Cocks & Houlbrook 2006).

This work concentrates on recovering historical people or events. As such, art, literature, film, TV and theatre are not included in detail, but the principals outlined here can be used to conduct research in those areas. Similarly, approaches in this book can be adapted to examine other sources that may not be addressed herein, such as Pinterest, Flickr and others.

The examples included reflect my research interests, but the principals can be used in any English-language source in any country.

Bibliography

Cocks, H. G. & Houlbrook, Matt (Eds.). (2006). *Palgrave Advances in the Modern History of Sexuality*. London: Palgrave Macmillan. doi:10.1057/9780230501805.

Cook, Matt. (2003). *London and the Culture of Homosexuality, 1885–1914*. Cambridge: Cambridge University Press.

Doan, Laura. (2013). *Disturbing Practices: History, Sexuality, and Women's Experience of Modern War*. Chicago: University of Chicago Press. doi:10.1093/tcbh/hwt035.

Foucault, Michel. (1980). *The History of Sexuality, Volume 1: An Introduction*. Translated by Robert Hurley. New York: Random House.

Shopland, Norena. (2017). *Forbidden Lives: LGBT Histories from Wales*. Bridgend, Wales: Seren Books.

Shopland, Norena & Leeworthy, Daryl. (2018). *Queering Glamorgan: A Research Guide to Sources for the Study of LGBT History*. Glamorgan Archives. Accessed online at https://glamarchives.gov.uk/wp-content/uploads/2018/08/Queering-Glamorgan-28Aug2018.pdf

Weeks, Jeffrey. (2000). *Making Sexual History*. Cambridge: Polity Press.

1 Dictionaries, word books and encyclopaedias

For the researcher, dictionaries, word books and encyclopaedias can be useful sources for checking the types and definitions of terminology used in the periods being researched. Many of these sources are freely available on the Internet. Some texts do not include words deemed 'unsavoury' at the time of publication, so researchers may have to sift through several volumes to find relevant references. Other limitations include the lack of references before the late nineteenth century to same-sex female terminology and the fact that gender diversity covers mainly hermaphrodites (intersex).

Before searching these sources, it is worth bearing in mind some of the limitations of digitised materials, such as the following:

The long s: ſ

The 'long s', or ſ, is a written and typed character that was used between the eighth century and the late 1790s. It was an elongated lower case 's' that came to resemble an 'f'. They cannot be recognised by optical character recognition (OCR) software. In publications featuring the 'long s', it is better to search pages individually rather than rely on a search engine.

Fonts and spellings

Some early dictionaries:

- use florid fonts - *Androgynous*
- split or hyphenate words to aid pronunciation – so'do'mite
- print the letters 'ae' together as æ – pæderaſty

The type used in historical texts can make it difficult for an OCR reader to identify words and characters. In such cases it is necessary to search directly for the required keywords.

In addition, spellings can be inconsistent. For example, androgynous can appear as androgynus, buggery as buggerie or pederasty as paederasty.

No results

When searching digitally in old books or documents, it is common to receive a 'no results' message. To test, search on a common word, such as 'and'. If there are still no results, then OCR is not working for that particular material.

In addition to being aware of how the form and formatting of historical texts can make searches difficult, researchers also must be sensitive to historical variations in terms used to identify or describe LGBTQIA+ individuals.

Women

Very few dictionaries include references to women's sexuality. The earliest known reference is from Thomas Blount's 1681 *Glossographia* under the definition of 'buggery':

Buggerie (Fr. Bougrerie) is defcribed to be *carnalis copula contra naturam, & bæcvel per confufionem Specterum, fe*, a man or a woman with a brute beaft; *vel fexuum*, a man with a man, or a woman with a woman. See *Levit. 10.22.23.* This offence committed with mankind or beaft, is Felony without Clergy; it being a fin againft God, Nature, and the Law; And, in antient time fuch offenders were to be burnt by the Common Law. *25 Hen.8.6. 5 Eliz. 17. Fitz. Nat. Br. 269.* My Lord *Coke* (Rep. 12. page 36.) faith, that this word comes from the *Italian, buggerare*, to bugger.

An earlier 1656 edition of the *Glossographia* does not include the female reference.

Although 'Sapphic' (and variations upon it) was a term used during the seventeenth century to describe same-sex love and relationships, general dictionaries and word books do not feature the term. Likewise, 'tribade' was used but does not appear in reference sources from the period. Both terms appear more regularly from the 1850s onwards.

1810 **A New and Enlarged Military Dictionary: In French and English** *by Charles James*

Tribade, *Fr.* a woman that has an unnatural attachment to one of her own sex; being the counterpart of a similar detestable crime among men; and both defeating the great ends of our creation. This creature, though suspected to exist in these islands, is not so generally known as she is upon the Continent of Europe, especially in France.

1846 Medical Lexicon: A Dictionary of Medical Science *by Robley Dunglison*

Tri'bas, gen. *Tri'badis*, (F.) *Tribade* … A female whose clitoris is so large as to cause her to be regarded as a hermaphrodite. One who acts as a male with another female or practices *tribadism*.

1827 Boyer's French Dictionary *by Abel Boyer*

Tribade – woman too familiar with a woman.

1850 A New Pocket Dictionary *by Thomas Nugent*

Tribade a woman who loves her own sex.

1854 Encyclopaedia Americana: A Popular Dictionary *by Francis Lieber*

Sappho, a distinguished Greek poetess … She is particularly accused of unnatural love to her own sex; hence the expression *Sapphic love*.

Although not used extensively, the terms 'tribade' and 'Sapphic' can be found in other nineteenth-century materials, such as the 1875 *Commentary on Paul's Letter to Romans* by Moses Easterly Lard:

The *Tribades*, a notorious class of women, addicted to one of the vices, practiced their crime under the name of Sapphic love; and every one at all read in history, has heard of the Lesbian vice. The same vice is said to be indulged in in Paris, France, in the present day; and there is little doubt of its existence in other modern cities.

Men

As would be expected, due to laws surrounding male same-sex activity, there are only a few common terms which dominate from the seventeenth century onwards. Although other terms do exist, such as 'virile love', 'love of males', 'male mingled love', these rarely surface.

Seventeenth century

1662 The New World of English Words *by Edward Phillips*

> A *Catamite*, (Lat.) an Ingle,[1] a boy kept for Sodomy.
> *Ganymed*, the son of *Tros*, whom for his excellent form, *Jupiter* fell in love with; and causing him to be brought up to Heaven upon an Eagles back, made him his Cup-bearer, instead of *Hebe* the daughter of *Juno*. Also, it is metaphorically taken for an Ingle, or boy hired to commit Sodomy.
> *Sodomitical*, (Lat.) belonging to *Sodomy*, i.e. buggery, or unnatural lust.
> *Pederastry*, or *Pæderasty*, (Greek) buggery, or a lusting after boyes.

Eighteenth century

A number of dictionaries and word books were published throughout the eighteenth century. Most that feature same-sex terms conform to the same definitions, so it will suffice to show just a few examples.

1706 The New World of Words: Or Universal English Dictionary *by John Kersey*

> Catamite, an Ingle, or Boy kept for sodomy.
> Pederast (Gr.) a Buggerer.
> Pederasty, a lusting after Boys, Sodomy, Buggery.
> Felony, (in Common Law) and Offence that in Degree next to Petty Treason, and comprehends divers Particulars, as Murder, Theft, killing of a Man's self, Sodomy, Rape, wilful firing of Houses, etc., which are all punish'd with Death, except *Petty Larceny*.
> Crista, a Crest, a Tuft, a Plume ... Cristae, are also certain knobs of Flesh that grow about the Fundament, and proceed from the filthy Act of Sodomy; the Roots of them being often chapt and cleft.
> Sodomit, one that commits Sodomy, a Buggerer.
> Sodomitical, belonging to that hainous [*sic*] Crime.
> Sodomy, Buggery, a Sin of the Flesh against Nature, so call'd because it was notoriously committed by the Inhabitants of the City of *Sodom*.
> Ingle, see *Catamite*.

1707 Glossographia Anglicana Nova *by Thomas Blount*

> *Buggery*, is a Copulation of Man or Woman with Brute Beasts; or of one Man with another.

1724 Cocker's English Dictionary *by Edward Cocker*

> *Sodomy*, Male-Venery, for which *Sodom* was destroyed.

Venery, meaning sexual indulgence, also appeared as 'Male-Venery', a term that can be equated with homosexuality. (Note that before the twentieth century nouns considered important were capitalised within texts, but using them, or not, will make no difference to the search). While not used widely, Male-Venery does appear occasionally in other publications of the eighteenth century, such as in the 'The Life of Bion' (a Greek philosopher) chapter in *The Lives of the Ancient Philosophers* (no author) of 1702:

> His discourses were full of Lewdness and Impiety. He was so much given to Male-Venery, especially with his own Scholars; that among all his auditors, not one would acknowledge himself to be his disciple.

'Male-Venery' also appears in *A Modest Defence of Publick Stews* (1740) by Phil Porney, Bernard Mandeville and George Ogle.

> *Polemo* was prosecuted by his Wife for Male Venery.
> *Crantor* made no Secret of his Love to his Pupil *Arcesilaus*.
> *Arcesilaus* made Love to *Demetrius* and *Leocharus*; the last, he said, he would fain have open'd; Besides, he openly frequented the two *Elean* Courtezans, *Theodota* and *Phileta*, and was himself enjoy'd by *Demochares* and *Pythocles*: He suffer'd the last, he said, for Patience-sake.
> *Bion* was noted for debauching his own Scholars.

A similar term is 'preposterous venery'[2] as featured in:

1703 The Short French Dictionary *by Guy Miège*

> Preposterous Venery, *Sodomie*.

1751 The Royal Dictionary Abridged: In Two Parts, French and English *by Abel Boyer*

> Pederastie (Sodomie) pederasty, sodomy, preposterous Venery, Buggery.

While not widely used, this can be found in some other publications, such as Owen and Johnston's *A New and General Biographical Dictionary* (1784). In the entry for the French poet Étienne Jodelle (1532–1573), the last line reads:

> He also wrote a poem against preposterous venery, or the sin of sodomy.

Other eighteenth-century terms can be found in local vernaculars or 'vulgar tongues', but most of these are rarely used.

1785 A Classical Dictionary of the Vulgar Tongue *by Francis Grose*

> Back Gammon Player. A sodomite.
> Indorser. A sodomite. To indorse with a cudgel; to drub or beat a man over the back with a stick, to lay *cane* upon Abel.
> Molly. A Miss Molly; an effeminate fellow, a sodomite.
> Twiddle-Poop. An effeminate looking fellow.
> Windward Passage. One who uses or navigates the windward passage; a sodomite.

Nineteenth century

The nineteenth century saw a profusion of dictionaries, word books and encyclopaedias, and when same-sex terms are included, they tend to appear in ways similar to the seventeenth and eighteenth centuries.

1806 The New and Complete American Encyclopedia

> BUGGERY, or SODOMY, is defined by Sir Edward Coke to be a carnal copulation against nature, either by a confusion of species, that is to say, wither a man or woman with a brute beast, or sexes, as a man with a man, or a man unnaturally with a woman.

1819 The Cyclopaedia *by Abraham Rees*

> Ganymede, a term lately come in use to express a catamite, or bardacio.[3] See SODOMY. The expression takes its rise from a young beautiful Trojan shepherd, thus called, whom Jupiter ravished, or carried off, by his eagle, or rather by himself, under the figure of an eagle ... Some say, that the Jupiter who ravished Ganymede was Tantalus, king of Phrygia; the eagle expressed the swiftness wherewith he was carried off.

1851 Dictionary of Dates, and Universal Reference *by Joseph Haydn*

> Sodom and Gomorrah. These cities, with all their inhabitants, destroyed by fire from heaven, 1897 B.C. *Bible; Blair; Usher.* The offence of sodomy was first sown in England by the Lombards. By our ancient law, the criminal was burnt to death, though Fleta says he should be burned alive. The crime was subject to ecclesiastical censure only at the time of Henry VIII, who made it felony without benefit of clergy, 1533. Confirmed by statute 5 Eliz., 1562.

Twentieth century

By the 1900s, terms coined in the late nineteenth century, such as 'homosexual', were beginning to appear more regularly.

1914 Stedman's Medical Dictionary *by Thomas Lathrop Stedman*

> homosexual [G. *Homos*, the same, + L. *sexus*, sex]. Relating to or possessing erotic attraction toward a person of the same sex. 2. A person attracted sexually to others of the same sex, an invert. homosexuality. A form of sexual perversion in which attraction exists for one of the same sex.

Welsh language

Of the three alternative languages in the UK, only Welsh-English dictionaries consistently include same-sex references, and most conform to the same definitions. Few of the Irish-English publications examined included terms, and no Scottish-English publications yielded results.

1832 A Dictionary of the Welsh Language *by William Owen Pughe*

Gwrrywgyd, Sodomy.
Gwrrywgydiaw, To commit sodomy.
Gwrrywgydiawl, Sodomitical.
Gwrrywgydiwr, A pederast.
Moçi, To wallow as swine; to commit sodomy.

1811 An English and Welsh Dictionary *by Thomas Jones*

Catamite, llangc at drin brynti; bryntwas, Sodom-was.
Sodomite, gwrryw-gydrwr.
Sodomitical, gwrrywgydiol.
Sodomy, *Buggery.*
Buggery, gwrryw-gydiad, sodomiaeth, anifeiligrwydd.

1864 An English-Welsh Pronouncing Dictionary *by Thomas Edwards*

Catamite, cydymaith, annaturiol, bryntwas, bryntlanc.

Irish

1864 An Irish-English Dictionary *by Edward O'Reilly*

Sodomach, a sodomite.
Sodomachd, sodomy.
Sodum, sodomy.

Other language dictionaries

Researching same-sex terminology through online dictionaries, word books and encyclopaedias can also lead to foreign language terminology.

1810 A New and Enlarged Military Dictionary: In French and English *by Charles James*

Dameret, *Fr.* a youth that affects feminine manners. An effeminate soft-speaking thing, which is sometimes seen in regimentals.

1854 A Dictionary of the Spanish and English Languages *by Giuseppe Marco Antonio Baretti and Mateo Seoane Sobral*

Sodomía, Sodomy, an unnatural crime.
Sodomíta, Sodomite, one who is guilty of sodomy.
Sodomítico, belonging to sodomy.

1864 A Romanized Hindustani and English Dictionary *by Nathaniel Brice*

Gándú, a catamite (see also Gánrú).
Laundábáz, a sodomite.
Laundábází, sodomy.
Táng dená, to hang up, to hang; to be a catamite.

1865 A Dictionary of the Hawaiian Language *by Lorrin Andrews*

Aikane. *v.* 1. To cohabit, as male with male, or female with female. 2. To commit sodomy; hence
Aikane. *s.* 1. An intimate friend of the same sex; a friend or companion of the same sex.
2. Those who mutually give and receive presents, being of the same sex.
3. Sodomy; dissoluteness of habit.
Moeaikane, *v. Moe* and *aikane*, sodomy. To commit sodomy.
Moeaikane, *s. Moe* and *aikane*, sodomy. Carnal abuse, male with male.

Gender diversity

Terms which can be related to the modern concept of gender diversity are rare in pre-twentieth-century dictionaries, word books and encyclopaedias. The most common term is 'hermaphrodite', which in modern times has been replaced by 'intersex'. Other terms are more ambiguous, and their inclusion or exclusion in gender diversity history is often the personal choice of the researcher or writer.

Hermaphrodite

1662 The New World of English Words *by Edward Phillips*

Hermaphrodite, (Greek) a word compounded of *Hermes*, i.e. *Mercury*, and *Aphrodite*, i.e. *Venus*, and signifieth [*sic*] one of both

Sexes, Man and Woman. See the story of *Hermaphroditus* and *Salmacis*, elegantly described in the fourth Book of Ovid's *Metamorphosis*.

1706 The New World of Words *by John Kersey*

Will-Jill, a sorry, inconsiderable Hermaphrodite.

1707 Glossographia Anglicana Nova *by Thomas Blount*

Hermaphrodite, one that is both Man and Woman.

1730 Dictionarium Britannicum *by Nathan Bailey*

A Scrat, an Hermaphrodite, one who is of both Sexes.
Will-Jill, a sorry, pitiful, inconsiderable Person, an Hermaphrodite.
Arsenothelys, an Hermaphrodite, a Beast which is both Male and Female.

1845 London Encyclopædia, or Universal Dictionary

ARSENOTHELYS, among ancient naturalists, the same with hermaphrodite. The Greeks use the word both in speaking of men and beasts.

1838 A Dictionary and Digest of the Law of Scotland *by William Bell*

HERMAPHRODITE. In the English law, a person partaking of both sexes may give, grant or inherit as either man or woman; *Tomlins' Dict.h.t.* Forbes, in his Institute, divides the sexes into male, female and 'hermaphrodite; *i.e.* both male and female, which is esteemed to be of that sex which is most prevailing in the person.' *Forbes, Inst. B. i. c. 1.*

Androgyny

1706 The New World of Words: Or Universal English Dictionary *by John Kersey*

Androgynus, one that is both Man and Woman, or has the Natural Parts of both Sexes; a Scrat or Will Jill, an effeminate Fellow.

1730 Dictionarium Britannicum *by Nathan Bailey*

> ANDROGYNUS, an Hermaphrodite who is both Man and Woman, having the natural Parts of both Sexes, a Will-Jill or Scrat.

Effeminate

1730 Dictionarium Britannicum *by Nathan Bailey*

> Smock-fac'd, effeminate, womanish of Countenance.
> GUSSET (in Heraldry) ... Mr *Guillim* calls it one of the whimsical Abatements[4] of Honour, for a Person who is either Lascivious, Effeminate, or a Sot, or all of them.

1771 Encyclopaedia Britannica

> GUSSET, in heraldry ... is an abatement of honour, denoting an effeminate person.

1794 A Dictionary of the English Language *by Samuel Johnson*

> To EFFEMINATE. To make womanish; to weaken; to emasculate; to unman.
> EFFEMINATION. The state of one grown womanish; the state of one emasculated or unmanned.

Other languages

1803 A Dictionary of the Welsh Language *by William Owen*

> Gwrwraig, gwrwreigez. A hermaphrodite.[5]
> Hivyn. A skin, a piece of skin. *Hivyn havog*, an hermaphrodite.[6]
> Mafwezwr. A light flutter; soft effeminate man.

1805 A Welsh-English Dictionary *by Titus Lewis*

> Hifyn, a skin; a piece of skin hifyn hafog, an hermaphrodite.

1832 A Dictionary of the Welsh Language Explained in English *by William Owen Pughe*

> Cydryw, hermaphrodite. a. congener, or homogeneous.[7]

1854 A Dictionary of the Spanish and English Languages *by Giuseppe Marco Antonio Baretti and Mateo Seoane Sobral*

> Hermafrodita, Hermafrodito. Hermaphrodite, androfyne, an animal or plant uniting two sexes.
> Andrógino. Hermaphrodite, an animal uniting both sexes, androgynus, androgyne.

1865 A Dictionary of the Hawaiian Language *by Lorrin Andrews*

> Mahu *s.* A man who assimilates his manners and dresses his person like a woman.[8]

Modern works

Hundreds of modern dictionaries and encyclopaedias are available online, for purchase or in libraries. Definitions vary. It is useful to check the publisher, as texts published by religious groups may provide negative definitions.

There are also hundreds of glossaries available on the internet that cover modern terminology. A useful site is *Homosaurus* by IHLIA LGBT Heritage, an internationally linked data vocabulary of LGBTQIA+ terms. *Homosaurus* is a companion to the broad subject term vocabularies used in the Library of Congress Subject Headings and by others.

Conclusion

Dictionaries, word books, encyclopaedias and similar works can be extremely useful for compiling glossaries. It is important, however, to understand the limitations of OCR software and online resources when examining works published prior to the nineteenth century.

Pre-nineteenth-century works indicate that there is a great deal of terminology available for researchers to use. Many terms from these texts do not appear in modern glossaries. Efforts by *Homosaurus* and others to compile new dictionaries are vital. Researchers who uncover new terms are encouraged to submit them for inclusion in LGBTQIA+ resources like *Homosaurus*.

Notes

1 An ingle, a paramour.
2 It was also a term used to describe infibulation in males when a clasp was placed through the foreskin.
3 A catamite.
4 An abatement on a coat of arms was a sign of dishonour.

5 Or, in some cases, such as the 1858 *An English and Welsh Dictionary* by Daniel Silvan Evans, a 'manly woman'.
6 *Hivyn havog* appears elsewhere with different spelling, for example in Titus Lewis's 1805 *A Welsh-English Dictionary.*
7 Cydryw, generally translated as 'of the same nature', was used in other Welsh dictionaries.
8 The term 'Mahu' is still used. According to an article by John Letman, a '33-year-old identifies as *mahu* – a gender role in traditional Hawaiian society that refers to people who exhibit both feminine and masculine traits' (Letman 2016).

Bibliography

Andrews, Lorrin. (1865). *A Dictionary of the Hawaiian Language.* Honolulu, HI: Henry M. Whitney. pp. 25, 368 & 394.

Anon. (1702). *The Lives of the Ancient Philosophers.* London: John Nicholson. p. 136.

Anon. (1771). *Encyclopaedia Britannica*, Vol. II. Edinburgh: A. Bell & C. MacFarquhar. p. 766.

Anon. (1806). *The New and Complete American Encyclopedia*, Vol. II. New York: John Low. p. 257.

Anon. (1845). *London Encyclopædia, or Universal Dictionary.* London: Thomas Tegg. p. 3.

Bailey, Nathan. (1730). *Dictionarium Britannicum: Or, a Complete Etymological English Dictionary.* London: T. Cox. n.p.

Baretti, Giuseppe Marco Antonio & Sobral, Mateo Seoane. (1854). *A Dictionary of the Spanish and English Languages*, Vol. 1. 11th ed. London: Longman, Brown and Co. p. 772.

Bell, William. (1838). *A Dictionary and Digest of the Law of Scotland.* Edinburgh: John Anderson. p. 469.

Blount, Thomas. (1681). *Glossographia: Or, A Dictionary Interpreting All Such Hard Words Now Used in Our Refined English Tongue.* London: The Newcomb. p. 95.

Blount, Thomas. (1707). *Glossographia Anglicana Nova.* London: D. Brown, T. Goodwin, T. Walthoe, et al. n.p.

Boyer, Abel. (1827). *Boyer's French Dictionary: Comprising All the Additions and Improvements of the Latest Paris and London Editions.* Boston, MA: T. Bedlington and Bradford & Peaslee. p. 511.

Boyer, Abel. (1751). *The Royal Dictionary Abridged: In Two Parts, French and English.* London: Messrs. Innys, Brotherton, Woodward, et al. n.p.

Brice, Nathaniel. (1864). *A Romanized Hindustani and English Dictionary.* London: Trübner & Co. pp. 181 & 316.

Cocker, Edward. (1724). *Cocker's English Dictionary.* London: T. Norris. n.p.

Dunglison, Robley. (1846). *Medical Lexicon: A Dictionary of Medical Science.* Philadelphia, PA: Lea and Blanchard.

Edwards, Thomas. (1864). *An English-Welsh Pronouncing Dictionary.* Treffynnon, Wales: P. M. Evans. p.190

Evans, Daniel Silvan. (1858). *An English and Welsh Dictionary*, Vol. 2. Denbigh, Wales: Thomas Gee. p. 302.

Grose, Francis. (1785). *A Classical Dictionary of the Vulgar Tongue*. London: S. Hooper. n.p.

Haydn, Joseph. (1851). *Dictionary of Dates, and Universal Reference*. London: Edward Moxon. p. 550.

IHLIA LGBT Heritage. (n.d.). *Homosaurus: An International LGBTQ Linked Data Vocabulary*. Accessed online at https://homosaurus.org

James, Charles. (1810). *A New and Enlarged Military Dictionary: In French and English*, Vol. 1. 3rd ed. London: T. Egerton.

Johnson, Samuel, (1794). *A Dictionary of the English Language*. 10th ed. London: T. Longman. n.p.

Jones, Thomas. (1811). *An English and Welsh Dictionary*. Denbigh, Wales: Thomas Gee. pp. 63, 52 & 416.

Kersey, John. (1706). *The New World of Words: Or Universal English Dictionary*. London: J. Phillips. n.p.

Lard, Moses Easterly. (1875). *Commentary on Paul's Letter to Romans*. Lexington, KY: Transylvania Printing and Publishing Company. p. 60.

Letman, Jon. (2016). 'Mahu Demonstrate Hawaii's Shifting Attitudes Toward LGBT Life.' *Aljazeera America*. 9 January.

Lewis, Titus. (1805). *A Welsh-English Dictionary*. Carmarthen, Wales: J. Evans. p. 178.

Lieber, Francis (ed.). (1854). *Encyclopaedia Americana: A Popular Dictionary*, Vol. 11. Boston, MA: B. B. Mussey & Co. p. 202.

Miège, Guy. (1703). *The Short French Dictionary*. 5th ed. The Hague: Henry van Bulderen. p. 16.

Nugent, Thomas. (1850). *A New Pocket Dictionary*, Vol. 1. No location: no publisher. p. 360.

O'Reilly, Edward. (1864). *An Irish-English Dictionary*. Dublin: James Duffy. p. 478.

Owen, William. (1803). *A Dictionary of the Welsh Language*, Vol. II. London: E. Williams. p. 194.

Owen, William & Johnston, William. (1784). *A New and General Biographical Dictionary*, Vol. 6. London: W. Strahan, T. Payne, et al. p. 405.

Phillips, Edward. (1662). *The New World of English Words*. London: E. P. n.p.

Porney, Phil, Mandeville Bernard & Ogle, George. (1740). *A Modest Defence of Publick Stews: Or, an Essay on Whoring*. London: A. Moore. p. v.

Pughe, William Owen. (1832). *A Dictionary of the Welsh Language Explained in English*. Denbigh, Wales: Thomas Gee. p. 279.

Pughe, William Owen. (1851). *A Dictionary of the Welsh Language*. Denbigh, Wales: Thomas Gee. pp.195 & 348.

Rees, Abraham. (1819). *The Cyclopaedia; or Universal Dictionary of Arts, Science and Literature*, Vol. XV. London: Longman. n.p.

Stedman, Thomas Lathrop. (1914). *Stedman's Medical Dictionary*. 3rd ed. New York: William Wood and Company. p. 421.

2 Lesbian and gay terminology

Dictionaries, word books and encyclopaedias set out terms used in a given era, but there was much more written which does not conform to a glossary. This chapter looks at terms and phrases that were used to describe what people were doing, such as *masquerading* or living *in disguise*, rather than labels for the people themselves. It also looks at how to greatly improve searching by combining words in order to take into account the individualistic writing styles of past authors. While 'lesbian' and 'gay' are modern terms, for the sake of expediency they are used in this chapter as content headings to organise information.

The sexologists who worked and wrote in the late nineteenth and early twentieth centuries developed a bewildering array of terms for all types of sex behaviour and sexuality. Researchers can consult their works (most of which are free to download) for additional terms. However, as many of the terms were not adopted outside of individual authors' writings, most are not included here.

Individuals were rarely named in newspaper articles written before the mid-nineteenth century to avoid bringing shame on them and their families. However, subsequently, the naming of individuals became increasingly more common. The researcher can look for them in other public records. Care is needed, however, as many people used aliases. While criminal records can provide a means to crosscheck some of these multiple identities, in many more cases individuals simply disappear.

Lesbian

Until the mid-twentieth century, there were only a handful of specific terms to describe same-sex activity and relationships between women. One of the most common is 'Sapphic'.

Sapphic

'Sapphic', 'sapphick', 'sapphism' and 'sapphists' were terms occasionally used from the seventeenth century onwards to describe same-sex love and relationships (not to be confused with the same words used to describe Sappho's style of poetry).[1] These terms do not usually appear as individual dictionary entries until the twentieth century, but they can occasionally be found in reference to Sappho:

1854 Encyclopaedia Americana: A Popular Dictionary *by Francis Lieber*

> Sappho, a distinguished Greek poetess ... She is particularly accused of unnatural love to her own sex; hence the expression *Sapphic love.*

The term is not used extensively. When it does appear, it is usually in a disapproving manner. Katherine Philips (c.1631–1664), the 'Welsh Sappho', who was the first English-language poet to evoke Sappho in verse, was called so in comparison to the style of poetry. However, much of her poetry concerned female same-sex love. After her death the poet Abraham Cowley (1618–1667), in his 1667 ode to Philips, sought to distance her from the association and 'shame' of Sappho's reputation:

> They talk of Sappho, but alas! the shame
>
> Ill Manners soil the lustre of her fame.
> (Cowley 1678, p. 4)

Sapphism could also mean an enlargement of the clitoris:

1855 Dictionary of Medical Terminology and Dental Surgery *by Chaplin A. Harris*

CLITORIS'MUS. An enlargement of the clitoris; also Sapphism.

Diaries and letters occasionally featured words such as 'Sapphic' or 'Sapphism'. For example, in her journals Hester Lynch Piozzi (1741–1821) described the Ladies of Llangollen – Eleanor Butler (1739–1829) and Sarah Ponsonby (1755–1831) – as 'damned Sapphists' (Piozzi 1952, p. 949). However, the terms were not generally used in works available to the general public until the words were reclaimed in the twentieth century.

Lesbian

Before the mid-nineteenth century, the term 'lesbian' was predominantly used to describe someone (or something, such as wine) that came from the island of Lesbos. It also appears as a ship's name. However, from the eighteenth century onwards, due to its association as the birth place of Sappho, it became more closely associated with same-sex relations between women. One of the earliest references is a fictional account of an individual called Myra:

1732 'An Ode to Myra' by William King (writing under the pseudonym Frederick Scheffer)

> Always whisper'd with a Sneer,
> When they Frow and thou art near.
> What if *Sappho* was so naught?
> I'll deny, that thou art taught
> How to pair the Female Doves,
> How to practise *Lesbian* Loves:
> But when little A—n's spread
> In her Grove or on thy Bed,
> I will swear, 'tis Nature's Call,
> 'Tis exalted Friendship all.
> (Scheffer 1732, p. 85)

In Book II King describes one of Myra's lovers:

> *Vrow pusilla*, or the little *Dutch* Frow, is the Wife of one *Traulus*. She's a Jewess and a Dwarf. However, this little Woman gave *Myra* more Pleasure than all the rest of her Lovers and Mistresses. She was therefore dignified with the Title of Chief of the *Tribades* or *Lisbians*.
> (Scheffer 1732, p. 56)

Joseph Lobdell, born in 1829, was the first American to be called a lesbian. Dr. P. M. Wise wrote about Lobdell in his 1883 'Case of Sexual Perversion' paper. However, Wise's definition would not be used today as Lobdell is now regarded as a transman.

During the feminist movements of the late nineteenth and early twentieth centuries, sexologists, such as Havelock Ellis and Iwan Bloch, expressed concerns about the growing number of women who were attracted to women. Although this was an issue of perception. As women's independence increased, women chose to share their lives with other women – and not all included a romantic element. In 1862 Francis Power Cobbe (1822–1904), herself in a relationship with Mary Lloyd (1819–1896), wrote that approximately 30 percent of women never married (Cobbe 1863).

The term 'pseudo-homosexuality', or 'pseudohomosexuality', was coined to separate women attracted to women from 'true inverts', although the term could also be used in regard to homosexual men and hermaphrodites. Female 'true inverts', who today would be called lesbians, were categorised by sexologists mainly in terms of masculinity. Those women who did not fit the masculine stereotype were referred to as 'pseudohomosexuals'. Sexologists often defined such women as having been seduced by the 'true invert' and, as such, were in a temporary state, or what Havelock Ellis called *spurious imitation*.

In 1921 an attempt was made to tighten up the 1885 Criminal Law Amendment Bill to include more protection for young girls being indecently assaulted as well as a clause intending to make all sexual activity between women illegal. The Bill in *Hansard* reads:

> Acts of indecency by females.
> Any act of gross indecency between female persons shall be a misdemeanour, and punishable in the same manner as any such act committed by male persons under section eleven of the Criminal Law Amendment Act, 1885.
>
> ('Lords Sitting: Commons Amendment' 1921)

However, there was a great deal of opposition to the Bill by the men in Parliament. At the time there were only two women MPs: Lady Astor and Countess Constance Markievicz, a Sinn Féin MP who refused to sit in the House of Commons. The Bill was not passed.

The Bill was intended as a 'spoiling amendment',[2] and lesbianism was not openly discussed in order to avoid informing or encouraging women. The Earl of Desart stated:

> I may perhaps draw cold comfort from the realisation that there are not many people who read the debates of either House. I am strongly of opinion that the mere discussion of subjects of this sort tends, in the minds of unbalanced people, of whom there are many, to create the idea of an offence of which the enormous majority of them have never even heard. I was going to say – I suppose I must not – that I know this does happen.
>
> ('Lords Sitting: Commons Amendment' 1921)

The terminology used during the debate was predominantly 'gross indecency', with the Earl of Malmesbury stating that it was a 'disgusting and polluting subject'. He claimed that 'this vice' would increase blackmail, it had been amplified by the war and 'all these unfortunate specimens of humanity exterminate themselves by the usual process'. There had been a previous attempt to criminalise same-sex activity between women in 1913, but the Home Secretary blocked it before it became an amendment.

Tribade

The word 'tribade' is frequently cited in twentieth-century texts when discussing historic female same-sex relations. The word developed from Greek *tribein* (to rub) via Latin *tribas* and eventually the French *tribade* in the early seventeenth century. However, it rarely appears prior to the twentieth century.

The word was combined with Sapphic terms, and lesbian was sometimes used to emphasise the point:

1875 Commentary on Paul's Letter to Romans *by Moses Easterly Lard*

> The *Tribades*, a notorious class of women, addicted to one of the vices, practiced their crime under the name of Sapphic love; and every one at all read in history, has heard of the Lesbian vice. The same vice is said to be indulged in in Paris, France, in the present day; and there is little doubt of its existence in other modern cities.

The quote above came from comments Lard was making about Biblical commentary on 'vile passions'.[3]

> [26]For this cause God gave them up unto vile affections: for even their women did change the natural use into that which is against nature:
> [27]And likewise also the men, leaving the natural use of the woman, burned in their lust one toward another; men with men working that which is unseemly, and receiving in themselves that recompence of their error which was meet.
> (Romans 1:26–27 King James Version)

Lard commented on the Romans text:

> They were the unnatural lusts which females cherished for females, and males cherished for males. It is impossible to conceive of

anything in the form of vice more disgusting than the practices to which they led. As the simple translation of the two verses presents their contents in a light sufficiently strong, I shall not comment on them in detail.

Lard also notes these were vices practiced by gentiles, thus assigning something considered unsavoury to another race or country: an example of the 'doesn't happen here' syndrome that is such a common feature in LGBTQIA+ history.

In *The Sexual Life of Our Time* (1906), Iwan Bloch wrote of female same-sex brothels:

> They have their parties, and even their balls, at which the virile tribades appear in men's clothing, and (as also when at home) use male nicknames. There also exist female prostitutes who devote their services entirely to urnindes. This tribadistic prostitution is especially widespread in Paris. Such prostitutes are called *gouines*, or *gourgnollies*, or *chevalières du clair du lune*. Theatrical agents are said to be especially occupied with tribadistic procurement. There also exist tribadistic brothels in Paris.
>
> (Bloch 1909, p. 530)

Tommy and Jack

'Tommy' is a word used at least from the eighteenth century to denote same-sex activity between women. The earliest known reference is from an anonymous satirical poem, *The Adulteress*, published in 1773:

> Women and Men, in these unnat'ral Times,
> Are guilty equal of unnat'ral crimes:
> Women with Woman act the Manly Part,
> And kiss and press each other to the heart.
> Unnat'ral Crimes like these my Satire vex;
> I know a thousand *Tommies* 'mongst the Sex:
> And if they don't relinquish such a Crime,
> I'll give their Names to be the scoff of Time.

However, 'Tommy' and another term, 'tabbies', were rarely employed as slang for lesbians. 'Jack' was sometimes used to denote masculine women, such as Anne Lister or 'Gentleman Jack', not just in the UK but also in the British colonies. A 1911 article in the *Barrier Miner*, an

Australian newspaper, discussed an unnamed cross-living woman, who was nicknamed Jack.

Other terms

In *Passions Between Women* (1993), Emma Donoghue suggests a number of euphemisms for same-sex activity and relationships between women used by various writers, such as *vicious irregularities, unaccountable intimacies, uncommon and preternatural lust, unnatural affections, unnatural appetites, game of flats* and *abominable and unnatural pollutions*. Again, these terms were not used frequently and did not always refer to women.

Publications available to the general public did not restrict themselves to those terms favoured by modern glossaries. Individuals write in individual ways. When researching or seeking same-sex relationships between women, it is advisable to look not for what they were, i.e., sapphists or lesbians, but for what they were doing. One of the most common ways to find these women is to look at instances of cross-dressing. Numerous women can be identified this way: women who passed as men, took male names, dressed as men and acted as men for periods ranging from a few months to whole lifetimes. Although in modern terminology many can be described as transmen, care has to be taken in assigning a modern term, as we cannot know in many of the cases whether the women considered themselves men or women.

Some terms can cross over, such as 'silent sin', which is often used for incest but may be used occasionally for homosexuality.

Disguise or masquerading

Newspaper headlines concerning cross-dressing or cross-living women in the past often included phrases centred on disguise. For example:

- 'female in disguise' – In an 1861 story in the *Pembrokeshire Herald*, Thomas Green, who worked as a mill hand and had 'for some time lived with another female' was described as a 'Female in Disguise'.
- 'disguised as a man' – After his death in 1906, Nicholas de Raylan was the subject of press coverage, including a 1907 *Weekly Mail* article entitled 'Woman's Three Wives' that reported he had left Russia 'disguised as a man', lived as such for many years and even married three times without the wives apparently being aware of Nicholas' biological sex.

Headlines also focused on performance or 'pretending to be a man.' For example, in 1833 the *Morning Chronicle* reported the story of Lavinia Edwards, also known as George Hamilton, who was tried for pretending to be a man and marrying fourteen wives. Alternatively, the word 'masquerade' was used. A popular form of headline centred on the concept of 'Masquerading in Male Attire', such as in an 1891 article from the *Western Mail*:

> A young Kentucky maiden has just been detected masquerading in male attire, and making love to the most attractive young women in the county adjoining the one in which she lived. When her sex was finally revealed it was ascertained that she had already been engaged to marry three farmers' daughters.

Similarly, a 1909 *Evening Express* headline announced 'Woman Marries Woman: Daring Masquerade at the Altar', and in 1910 the *Evening Express* ran a story with the headline 'Dressed as a Man: Girl Masquerades for Ten Years':

> Taking a pipe from her pocket. Miss Gray, who is in outward appearance a handsome youth of nineteen, asked the magistrate if her arrest was due to information laid by 'a woman twice my age,' of Newark Valley, New York. 'That woman,' she added, 'fell in love with me and insisted on marriage. She told me that if I would not she would make my whole life hideous for me. She has almost succeeded!'

Female husband

The term 'female husband' first appeared in 1746 in Henry Fielding's *The Female Husband*, a book based on newspaper reports from the same year about Mary/Charles Hamilton. The term appeared frequently in the eighteenth and nineteenth centuries until its use abated in the late nineteenth century, although there are a few examples up until the 1910s.

A great deal has been written about female husbands, but many reproduce the same stories of well-known individuals. Stories about less-known women can be found using variations of search terms, such as *woman marrying a woman, women marrying women* or *marrying her own sex*.

A *Bristol Times and Mirror* piece from 1872 entitled 'A Woman Marrying a Woman', about an unnamed individual from Edinburgh, makes a rare comment that she 'fell in love with a young woman'. In most cross-dressing cases, the one cross-dressing is described as 'making love to' another individual, an old phrase for what we would now consider flirting or wooing. 'Gallanting a lass' is another expression used to describe cross-dressing individuals' actions.

Gay men

Gay

The word 'gay' as a reference to sexual orientation is a relatively modern term. It dates back to the late nineteenth century, although it became more popular in the mid-twentieth century. It was adopted in preference to the more scientific term 'homosexual'. The main difficulty with using the word as a search term is that returns will include forenames and surnames as well as instances of its other definitions, such as 'joyful', 'happy' and the like. From the seventeenth century onwards, the word 'gay' was linked to immorality, people living a 'loose life' and prostitutes. It is believed that its link to male prostitution was the reason the term became associated with homosexuality.

Effeminate

Today the word 'effeminate' tends to conjure up images of a certain type of man. Modern dictionaries reinforce these images with synonyms, such as womanish, unmanly, effete, foppish, affected, mincing or posturing. For the most part, 'effeminate' is used as a derogatory term – women were historically considered weaker than men, and the comparison was seen as acceptable in the past. 'Effeminate' was used in a variety of contexts, such as in the case of Marged ferch Ifan (1696–1793). As I discussed in *Forbidden Lives*, legitimate questions can be asked with regard to her sexual orientation and her gender identity. Marged was said to have married 'the most effeminate of her admirers'. As most of Marged's fame rested on her extreme masculinity, the word may well have been used to emphasise the difference in their bodily strength – or, as the *Carmarthen Journal* noted in 1811, 'as if determined to maintain that superiority which nature had bestowed upon her'. The record leaves us unable to make any comments about the partners' sexual orientation or gender identity.

'Effeminate' could also be used to describe 'weakness of will' or softness:

1864 Walker and Webster Combined in a Dictionary of the English Language *by John Longmuir*

> SOFT, *a*. Easily yielding to pressure; gentle; easy; effeminate; delicate; impressible; undisturbed; mild to the eye; not glaring; mild; warm; timorous; tender; kind.

As can be seen from the previous chapter, effeminate can also be found in conjunction with sodomy:

1785 A Classical Dictionary of the Vulgar Tongue *by Francis Grose*

> Molly. A Miss Molly; an effeminate fellow, a sodomite.

The term can also be associated with gender diversity:

1706 The New World of Words *by John Kersey*

> Androgynus [*sic*], one that is both Man and Woman, or has the Natural Parts of both Sexes; a Scrat or Will Jill, an effeminate Fellow.

Caution therefore needs to be practiced when 'effeminate' is used in reference to a man prior to the twentieth century. It is not until after the mid-nineteenth century that effeminate becomes more closely linked to descriptions of men.

Sodomy, buggery and gross indecency

'Sodomy' is a word adapted from the Biblical story in Genesis (chapters 18–20) regarding the cities of Sodom and Gomorrah. Two angels were staying with Lot when his house was surrounded by men who demanded to 'know' them, a term which often included a sexual element. Lot offered his two virgin daughters as an alternative. Lot's willingness for them to be raped has never been castigated in the same way as the men's supposed intention to rape the angels. Throughout history the rape of women has rarely been treated as harshly as sodomy between two men.

From mediaeval times onwards, the word 'sodomy' has been used to indicate penetrative anal sex between men and women, but more frequently between two men. It could also (and still does in some countries today) refer to bestiality.

'Buggery' was first used in law in the Buggery Act 1533 during the reign of Henry VIII. This was the first time the terms 'sodomy' or 'buggery' were used in the civil, rather than the ecclesiastical, courts. It was described as a vice committed with mankind or beast. From 1716 it also applied to heterosexual sodomy, although heterosexual acts of buggery were rarely prosecuted with the same frequency as homosexual buggery. Due to low conviction rates, as evidence of semen was required, the act was repealed in 1828 by section 1 of the Offences Against the Person Act, which required only evidence of penetration. Buggery remained a capital offence until 1861, although the last man to be executed was hanged in 1835. Once the capital penalty was removed, the crime was redefined under the Offences Against the Person Act 1861 as:

Unnatural Offences: Sodomy and Bestiality.
61 Whosoever shall be convicted of the abominable Crime of Buggery, committed either with Mankind or with any Animal, shall be liable, at the Discretion of the Court, to be kept in Penal Servitude for Life or for any Term not less than Ten Years.

Unnatural Offences: Attempt to commit an infamous Crime.
62 Whosoever shall attempt to commit the said abominable Crime, or shall be guilty of any Assault with Intent to commit the same, or of any indecent Assault upon any Male Person, shall be guilty of a Misdemeanour, and being convicted thereof shall be liable, at the Discretion of the Court, to be kept in Penal Servitude for any Term not exceeding Ten Years and not less than Three Years, or to be imprisoned for any Term not exceeding Two Years, with or without Hard Labour.

(HM Government 1861)

Buggery remained a crime in the UK until the law was repealed in 1967, however it still exists in a number of other countries.

As a number of cases concerning sodomy and buggery failed to be proven due to the exact nature of the proof required, the crime of *gross indecency* was introduced in Section 11 of the Criminal Law Amendment Act 1885, popularly known as the Labouchere Amendment. This offence was added to sodomy, and the combination criminalised any sexual relationships between men, but not women. It was under this Act that Oscar Wilde was prosecuted in 1895 and Alan Turing was prosecuted in 1952.

The Labouchere Amendment also became known as the blackmailer's charter. It made it easier to accuse someone of gross indecency. Of course, blackmailing over sexuality had existed earlier, as illustrated by an 1808 *York Herald* article on the York Lent Assizes:

> Francis Brown of Kellythrope ... it appeared that Mr. Brown had indicted Paul and Eskritt, at the Midsummer Sessions, 1807, for a conspiracy to extort money from him, upon a false charge of Sodomy.

Care needs to be exercised when using the term 'gross indecency'. It could mean many things, and its interpretation was often up to the arresting officer and/or the courts. However, using the search terms 'Section 11' or 'Criminal Law Amendment Act' can produce results, such as an 1896 article titled 'Shocking Charge Against a Minister' in the *South Wales Daily Post*:

> At the North London Police-court on Tuesday the Rev. Francis George Widdows, minister of the Martin Luther Church, Hackney, and formerly a monk, was again charged with an offence under section 11 of the Criminal Law Amendment Act.

Homosexual

Carl Westphal (1833–1890) is credited with giving birth to the concept that homosexuality was not 'a category of forbidden acts' but something more innate in his 1870 paper on 'contrary sexual sensations' (Foucault 1980, p. 42). Detailing the case of a young woman, Westphal believed her sexual attraction to women was congenital and not a vice.

The idea that homosexuality was inborn had existed for some time before Westphal's paper. He had himself been influenced by the writings of Karl Heinrich Ulrichs (1825–1895), who was 'sexually inverted'. From 1864 Ulrichs wrote on homosexuality, came out to his family as an 'urning' and wrote twelve books, the last being *Forschungen über das Rätsel der mannmännlichen Liebe* (*Studies on the Riddle of Male-Male Love*) (1870), which argued that same-sex love was natural. He coined the words 'Urning' (English: 'Uranian') for men who desired men and 'Urningin' for women who desired women. Ulrichs, who was the first person whose sexual orientation can be described as homosexual, publicly spoke in defence of same-sex relations at the 1867 Congress of German Jurists in an attempt to revise the laws against same-sex love. He did not succeed but continued his attempts in later years.

Ulrichs' terms were used by others, such as Krafft-Ebing in *Psychopathia Sexualis*:

Careful observation among the ladies of large cities soon convinces one that homosexuality is by no means a rarity. Uranism may nearly always be suspected in females wearing their hair short, or who dress in the fashion of men, or pursue the sports and pastimes of their male acquaintances; also in opera singers and actresses, who appear in male attire on the stage by preference.

(Krafft-Ebing 1894, p. 398)

Following the writings of Ulrichs, Westphal and others, the study of sexuality in all its forms – sexology – became popular in the late nineteenth century. Sexologists coined a bewildering array of terms, although most of them were never adopted. In addition, many of the sexologists' descriptions were written in Latin to keep sensitive material away from lay people.

The one term which did come to dominate same-sex sexology was 'homosexual'/'homo-sexual'. As Havelock Ellis wrote, it was

devised (by a little-known Hungarian doctor, Benkert, who used the pseudonym Kertbeny) in the same year (1869), but at first attracted no attention. It has, philologically, the awkward disadvantage of being a bastard term compounded of Greek and Latin elements, but its significance – sexual attraction to the same sex – is fairly clear and definite, while it is free from any question-begging association of either favorable or unfavorable character. (Edward Carpenter has proposed to remedy its bastardly linguistic character by transforming it into 'homogenic'; this, however, might mean not only 'toward the same sex,' but 'of the same kind,' and in German already possesses actually that meaning.) The term 'homosexual' has the further advantage that on account of its classical origin it is easily translatable into many languages. It is now the most widespread general term.

(Ellis 1900)

Karl-Maria Kertbeny (1824–1882) was himself homosexual.

As Michel Foucault famously put it in *The History of Sexuality* (1980), homosexuality was 'defined by the ancient civil or canonical codes, sodomy was a category of forbidden acts ... The sodomite had been a temporary aberration;[4] the homosexual was now a species':

The nineteenth-century homosexual became a personage, a past, a case history and a childhood, in addition to being a type of life, a life form and a morphology, with an indiscreet anatomy and possibly a mysterious physiology. Nothing that went into his total composition was unaffected by his sexuality. It was everywhere present in him.

By the early twentieth century the belief that homosexuality was a congenital sexual attraction started to take hold:

1914 Stedman's Medical Dictionary *by Thomas Stedman*

homosexual [G. *Homos*, the same, + L. *sexus*, sex]. Relating to or possessing erotic attraction toward a person of the same sex. 2. A person attracted sexually to others of the same sex, an invert. homosexuality. A form of sexual perversion in which attraction exists for one of the same sex.

The acceptance of homosexuality as a sexual orientation did not take hold until the mid-twentieth century.

Other terms

In publications available to the masses, the terms 'sodomy' and 'buggery' were rarely used. Instead, they were covered by a variety of euphemisms often adopted according to an individual writer's preference or a particular publication's style. Descriptions regarding men who were arrested for gross indecency include: *unnatural offence, disgusting offence, unnatural crime, abominable crime, detestable crime, against the order of nature, indecent conduct* and *indecent exposure. Unfit for publication* is also a good indicator, although, as with all the terms listed above, it could cover many offences.

Much depends on the patience of the researcher, who must determine how much retrieved material to retain for future use. Many of the cases cannot be verified as same-sex activity until archival records are examined. For example, an 1882 piece in *The Cambrian* gives no indication as to the nature of the defendant's 'unnatural offence' (Figure 2.1).

By consulting the arrest records, it becomes apparent that the charge is buggery (Figure 2.2).

When researching cases in archives it is necessary to bear in mind that there were individuals who did not care to write out the word 'buggery' in full. As such, the word can appear as 'b—y' (Figure 2.3) or 'b'gg'y' (Figure 2.4).

The nature of an offense may only become apparent after further research. For example, an 1859 piece from the *Cardiff & Merthyr Guardian* on Denis Ryan was recovered using the search term *unmentionable offence* (Figure 2.5). However, when checked against the Glamorganshire Assizes records, it transpires that Ryan was charged with 'carnally knowing a certain female donkey'.

GLAMORGANSHIRE SUMMER ASSIZES.

CRIMINAL COURT.—Friday.
[Before Baron Huddlestone.]
UNNATURAL OFFENCES.

Antonio Baradchi, 28, a Greek sailor, was indicted for committing a detestable and abominable crime on board the brigantine Annie, in the South Docks, Swansea, on the 10th February last. The case was heard at the last Assizes at Cardiff, but the jury being unable to agree, after being locked up for several hours, they were discharged, and the prisoner was remanded for trial to the present Assizes. Mr. D. Lewis now prosecuted. The prisoner was undefended, and he pleaded "not guilty." The jury found him guilty of the attempt, and he was sentenced to two years' imprisonment with hard labour. The prosecutor's expenses were disallowed.

Figure 2.1 'Glamorganshire Summer Assizes.' (1882). *The Cambrian.* 11 August. p. 7.

Feloniously, wickedly, diabolically, and against the order of nature, did beat, wound and illtreat one Joseph McLean with intent to commit and perpetrate that detestable and abominable crime (not to be named among Christians) called buggery, at Swansea, on the 10th day of February, 1882

Figure 2.2 Glamorgan Archives, Q/S/C/5 – Calendar of Prisoners, 1882–1888.

On the 3rd April, 1897, at Barry, unlawfully committing an un-natural offence with another male person, named Henry Walter Antcliff.

1st July | Ditto | · · Guilty of b———y.

Figure 2.3 Glamorgan Archives, Q/S/C/7 – Calendar of Prisoners, 1895–1902.

Feloniously committing the abo-minable crime of b'gg'y with Richard John Green, on the 2nd December, 1899, at Ystradyfodwg.

Figure 2.4 Glamorgan Archives, Q/S/C/7 – Calendar of Prisoners, 1895–1902.

MERTHYR.—Denis Ryan, 27, labourer, charged with an unmentionable offence, at Merthyr, on the 1st September. Mr. T. Allen appeared for the prosecution. The prisoner, who was undefended, was found Guilty. Judgment of Death was recorded against the prisoner.

Figure 2.5 'Glamorganshire Winter Assizes.' (1859). *Cardiff & Merthyr Guardian*. 17 December. p. 6.

Conclusion

It was not until the more open discussions of sexuality in late nine-teenth century that the language of sexual orientation and gender identity became more complex. The sexual orientation of women was largely described by just a handful of terms. By turning to broader descriptions of cross-dressing or cross-living, it is possible to locate those women we would today regard as lesbian or transmen. The range of terminology for men's sexual orientation is much greater. There is a bewildering array of terms, which allows for multiple possibilities when searching for material. Researchers should not restrict themselves to only those terms which appear in glossaries.

Notes

1 William King, writing under the pseudonym Frederick Scheffer (1732), uses the word 'sapphoic', but he seems to be the only one to do so.
2 An amendment intended to wreck a bill. Similarly, MP Tim Loughton attempted to wreck the Marriage (Same Sex Couples) Bill in 2003 by claiming Civil Partnerships should also be made available for heterosexual couples, which came about in 2019.
3 'Vile passions' was a term which could and did mean many things.
4 Although some, such as Rictor Norton, claim the translation is more accurate as 'temporary sinner' rather than 'temporary aberration' (Norton 2010).

Bibliography

'1885 Labouchere Amendment.' [Criminal Law Amendment Act] (1885). *UK Parliament*. Accessed online at https://www.parliament.uk/about/living-heritage/transformingsociety/private-lives/relationships/collections1/sexual-offences-act-1967/1885-labouchere-amendment

Anon. (1773). *The Adulteress*. London. pp. 26–27.

'A Woman Marrying a Woman.' (1872). *Bristol Times and Mirror*. 9 January. p. 3.

Bloch, Iwan. (1909). *The Sexual Life of Our Time in Its Relations to Modern Civilization*. London: Rebman. p. 530.

'Carmarthen: March 23, 1811.' (1811). *Carmarthen Journal*. 23 March. p. 3.

Cobbe, Francis Power. (1863). 'What Shall We Do with Our Old Maids.' In *Essays on the Pursuits of Women*. London: Emily Faithful. p. 59. Accessed online at https://archive.org/details/essaysonpursuit00cobbgoog

Cowley, Abraham. (1678). *The Works of Mr. Abraham Cowley*. 5th ed. London. p. 4.

Donoghue, Emma. (1993). *Passions Between Women: British Lesbian Culture 1668–1801*. London: Scarlet Press.

'Dressed as a Man: Girl Masquerades for Ten Years.' (1910). *Evening Express*. 22 January. p. 2.

Ellis, Havelock. (1900). *Studies in the Psychology of Sex, Volume 2: Sexual Inversion*. Kindle ed. E-text prepared by Juliet Sutherland and the Project Gutenberg Online Distributed Proofreading Team. Kindle location 10.

Foucault, Michel. (1980). *The History of Sexuality, Volume 1: An Introduction*. Translated by Robert Hurley. New York: Random House. pp. 42–43.

'General Intelligence: A Female in Disguise.' (1861). *Pembrokeshire Herald*. 10 May. p. 3.

'Glamorganshire Summer Assizes.' (1882). *The Cambrian*. 11 August. p. 7.

'Glamorganshire Winter Assizes.' (1859). *Cardiff & Merthyr Guardian*. 17 December. p. 6.

Grose, Francis. (1785). *A Classical Dictionary of the Vulgar Tongue*. London: S. Hooper. n.p.

Harris, Chaplin A. (1855). *Dictionary of Medical Terminology and Dental Surgery*. 2nd ed. Philadelphia, PA: Lindsay & Blakiston. p. 162.

HM Government. (1861). Offences Against the Person Act. London: HM Government. Section 61 & 62.

Kersey, John. (1706). *The New World of Words: Or Universal English Dictionary*. London: J. Phillips. n.p.

Krafft-Ebing, Richard von (1894). *Psychopathia Sexualis*. Translated by F. J. Rebman. New York: Rebman Company. p. 398.

Lard, Moses Easterly. (1875). *Commentary on Paul's Letter to Romans*. Lexington, KY: Transylvania Printing and Publishing Company. p. 60.

Lieber, Francis (Ed.). (1854). *Encyclopaedia Americana: A Popular Dictionary*, Vol. 11. Boston, MA: B. B. Mussey & Co. p. 202.

Longmuir, John. (1864). *Walker and Webster Combined in a Dictionary of the English Language*. London: William Tegg. p. 434.

'Lords Sitting: Commons Amendment.' (1921). *Hansard* vol. 43, ser. 5. 15 August. cc. 567–577.

'Masquerading in Male Attire.' (1891). *Western Mail*. 4 September. p. 5.

Norton, Rictor. (2010). *F*ck Foucault: How Eighteenth-Century Homosexual History Validates the Essentialist Model*. UCLA Mellon Sawyer Seminar: Homosexualities, From Antiquity to the Present. 27 May. Accessed online at https://harringtonparkpress.com/download/Norton.F_ck-Foucault.pdf

Piozzi, Hester Lynch. (1951). *Thraliana: The Diary of Mrs. Hester Lynch Thrale (Later Mrs. Piozzi), 1776–1809*. 2nd ed. Edited by Katherine C. Balderston. Vol. 2. p. 949. Scheffer, Frederick [William King]. (1732). 'An Ode to Myra.' In *The Toast, an Epic Poem in Four Books*, Book II. Translated by Peregrine O'Donald. Dublin. pp. 56 & 85.

'Shocking Charge Against a Minister.' (1896). *South Wales Daily Post*. 28 July. p. 3.

Shopland, Norena. (2017). *Forbidden Lives: LGBT Stories from Wales*. Bridgend, Wales: Seren Books. p. 17.

Stedman, Thomas. (1914). *Stedman's Medical Dictionary*. 3rd ed. New York: William Wood and Company. p. 421.

'The Case of the Person called Lavina Edwards.' (1833). *Morning Chronicle*. 2 February. p. 4.

'The Woman Dressed in Male Attire.' (1911). *Barrier Miner*. 3 November. p. 6.

Ulrichs, Karl Heinrich. (1870). *Forschungen über das Rätsel der Mannmännlichen Liebe*. Leipzig: Max Spohr.

Wise, P. M. (1883). 'Case of Sexual Perversion.' *Alienist and Neurologist*, vol. 4. pp. 87–91.

'Woman Marries Woman: Daring Masquerade at the Altar.' (1909). *Evening Express*. 15 June. p. 4.

'Woman's Three Wives.' (1907). *Weekly Mail*. 5 January. p. 3.

'York Lent Assizes, 1808.' (1808). *York Herald*. 12 March. p. 3.

3 Bisexual and other sexual orientations terminology

As with the words 'lesbian' and 'gay', 'bisexual' is predominantly a modern term, but for expediency it will be used in this work.

From the late twentieth century to modern times, the most common shortcut for describing sexual orientation and gender diversity is through the use of the acronym LGBT (lesbian, gay, bisexual and transgender). However, because it leaves no room for other orientations, such as asexual, the term now includes a + sign to indicate the inclusion of all sexualities and gender diversities (LGBT+). In this work I have adopted the acronym LGBTQIA+, which takes into account queer, intersex and asexual people. With the ongoing addition of even more orientations and their associated letters, the acronym has become something often described as 'alphabet soup'.

Many of the sexualities included in modern glossaries, such as *pansexual, polysexual, androsexual, gynosexual* and others, are not found in historical sources. As such, only those terms which appear regularly, namely 'bisexual' and 'asexual', are included here. Historic writings are not always obliging in the use of the terms that we currently use, so it is necessary to look elsewhere for words that may disguise same-sex relationships, such as 'inverts', a term which had multiple meanings, or 'romantic friendships'.

For a comprehensive list of modern terms, the Moscas de Colores website (2020) features a *Gay Dictionary* compiled from 68 languages, a *Lesbian Dictionary* from 24 languages and a modern LGBT+ Glossary.

Bisexual

The word 'bisexual', or 'bi-sexual', is used in botany to describe flowers with both male and female reproductive structures. In zoology it often appears in conjunction with the word 'hermaphrodite' to describe some invertebrates, fish and certain mammals, such as hyenas.

Until the twentieth century, bisexual might be used merely to indicate binary genders, such as in an 1894 piece in the *South Wales Daily News* about a bi-sexual ghost:

There is a Norfolk ghost … it haunts a farmhouse in the neighbourhood of Norwich … it appears now as a man, now as a woman, or rather that the dread mysterious figure has a certain bi-sexual character.

It was not until the late nineteenth and early twentieth century that the word began to be used to denote an individual who engaged in sexual activity with both female and male partners. Otto Weininger wrote in 1903:

there are no inverts who are completely sexually inverted. In all of them there is from the beginning an inclination to both sexes; they are, in fact, bisexual. It may be later on they may actively encourage a slight leaning toward one sex or the other, and so become practically unisexual either in the normal or inverted sense, or surrounding influence may bring about this result for them.

(Weininger 1907, p. 48)

However, the idea of a person being attracted to both sexes did exist previously. Ulrich, who coined a raft of words for varying sexualities, used *Uranodioninge* to denote those attracted to more than one gender.

The word 'bisexual' was used sporadically until 1920, when Sigmund Freud (1962) coined the term 'innate bisexuality' (Freud 1962). Freud based this on work done by Wilhelm Fliess, who believed that humans went through monthly cycles of sexuality. Freud's theory was that people were born bisexual but evolved (through various influences) to heterosexuality, with bisexuality being a latent state. This theory was taken up in 1922 by Wilhelm Stekel in *Bi-Sexual Love: The Homosexual Neurosis*, alongside other writers such as William James, who stated: 'There is no inborn heterosexuality and no inborn homosexuality. There is only bisexuality.'

Emile Laurent, who studied 'bisexual manifestations' in the late nineteenth century, coined the term 'psychic hermaphroditism' to describe bisexuals – but, like many of the terms used by the sexologists, it never became popular as (like many of the other terms) it was ambiguous (Laurent 1894, p. 211). It could mean bisexuality or homosexuality. Eventually it became more associated with individuals who were considered morphologically one sex but psychologically the other.

The association of bisexuality with hermaphroditism can still be seen in the late twentieth century:

1976 The Concise Oxford Dictionary *edited by J. B. Sykes*

> bīsĕ'xūal *a*. Of two sexes; having both sexes in one individual; (of person); sexually attracted by members of both sexes.

Despite a lack of terminology to research bisexual people, it should be borne in mind that most people throughout history were required to get married, and any same-sex activity which has been designated gay or homosexual by modern historians could, or perhaps should, be more accurately described as sexually fluid. Because using the word bisexual to denote a sexual orientation did not become popular until the mid-twentieth century, it cannot be used to describe individuals from the past.

Asexual

The term 'asexual', like bisexual, originated from descriptions of flora and certain classes of animals. It indicates those that could sexually reproduce by themselves and has been in use since the eighteenth century.

With regard to humans, 'asexual' was used occasionally as a term to describe someone with no genitals or someone of undetermined sex. An 1875 article on 'Population Statistics of the German Empire' in the *Glasgow Herald* specified that 'one child is described as asexual'.

Definitions of 'asexual' also include a lack of sexual attraction to others or low/absent sexual activity, although in this context the word itself may not be employed. References, therefore, may be found by using search terms concerning *sexual attraction, sexless* or *non-sexual*, such as the following piece discussing menstruation (note the use of the word 'creatures'):

1867 Obstetrics: The Science and the Art *by Charles Delucena Meigs*

> Some women are to be met with who never menstruate ... Among these exceptional creatures are to found those in whom the ovaria or the uterus has never been developed. Dr. Renauldin, on the 28th of Feb. 1826, reported to the Royal Academy of Medicine the

case of a woman who died at the age of fifty-two years. She never had any appearance of menstruation. The breasts were not developed. She had only a cervix uteri, which was the size of a writing-quill – there was no womb proper – and the ovaries were scarcely developed. Such a woman could not menstruate because of the double failure of uterus and ovary. There could be no sexual passion; indeed, such a creature was scarcely sexual ... There are numerous examples of females who did never menstruate, owing to the absence of the ovaries. When our domestic animals are subjected to the operation of spaying, they are totally deprived of the power of ovulation; and with its loss the sexual sense disappears as well as the sexual attraction also; or if any remains are discernible, they are very imperfect.

It is also possible that a number of cases discussed by sexologists of the late nineteenth and early twentieth centuries that refer to *frigidity* in women may actually be referring to asexuality.

Bisexuality was used in this context in the Kinsey Scale of 1948. This now outdated measure, devised by doctors Alfred Kinsey, Wardell Pomeroy and Clyde Martin and published in *Sexual Behavior in the Human Male* (1948), was intended to show that people did not fit exclusively into a binary heterosexual or homosexual category. However, the scale did include an 'X' category for those individuals who had no socio-sexual contacts or sexual attractions, and modern interpretations of the scale have relabelled the X category as asexual.

The word 'asexual' was also used interchangeably with 'hermaphrodite' to describe strong, independent women, particularly from the rise of the women's movement from the 1830s onwards. It was often used in discussions of women's suffrage, women's fight to wear trousers or women taking up sports, as in this condemnatory *Daily Mail* piece:

1903 'The Deterioration of Women' by J. H. Harrison, et al.

The modern girl begins early, and continues till her marriage, and often afterwards, the unnatural athletics which ruin her figure and frequently her health. She shoots up tall, flat-chested, colourless, and lacking in reasonable proportions. Wried [*sic*] and atrophied by rough wear and unseemly habits, that delicate form shrinks and withers from the norm of health and beauty. No longer had our girls the pleasant contours and healthy lines of muliebrity.[1] They tend to become asexual, and to conform to a standard which is not theirs but man's.

'Asexual' as a term used to describe a sexual orientation does not come into use until the mid-twentieth century.

Invert

In 1869 Karl Westphal coined the phrase *congenital invert*, believing that sexual inversion was a natural condition. However, at first the term was closely allied to women with a masculine appearance, rather than same-sex sexual attraction or relationships.

Sexual inversion was, according to Havelock Ellis, a term which had originated in Italy, but it had been used in 1882 by the influential French psychiatrists Jean-Martin Charcot and Valentin Magnan, who argued that all forms of inversion and perversion were caused by physical, psychic and moral degeneracy.

The concept of inversion as congenital was adopted by many of the famous sexologists. Havelock Ellis wrote in *Studies in the Psychology of Sex* (1900):

> It could not be positively affirmed of all such persons that they were born inverted, but in most the inverted tendency seems to be instinctive, and appears at a somewhat early age. In any case, however, it must be realized that in this volume we are not dealing with subjects belonging to the lunatic asylum, or the prison. We are concerned with individuals who live in freedom.

By the early twentieth century, as the word 'homosexual' was becoming the dominant term, invert was still being used as a synonym.

1914 A Practical Medical Dictionary *by Thomas Lathrop Stedman*

> homosexual [G. *Homos*, the same, + L. *sexus*, sex]. Relating to or possessing erotic attraction toward a person of the same sex. 2. A person attracted sexually to others of the same sex, an invert.

Published in 1928, *The Well of Loneliness*, a novel by Radclyffe Hall (1880–1943), featured an inverted character. Hall, herself an invert, wrote the book because she wanted to publicise the sexologists' work, which had previously been confined to medical text books. She described her work as 'the first long and very serious novel entirely upon the subject of sexual inversion'. Havelock Ellis wrote in a 'Commentary' at the beginning of the book, 'it is the first English novel which presents, in a completely faithful and uncompromising form, various aspects of sexual inversion as it exists among us today'. The book was banned until 1949. When it did reappear Ellis's 'Commentary' had been removed, and it is not included in any subsequent editions.

Romantic friendships vs. same-sex relationships

Today 'bromance' has become common parlance, describing male relationships like those of Smithy and Gavin in the popular TV sitcom *Gavin and Stacey*. Similarly, 'womance' or 'sismance' are used in reference to *Sex in the City*. Certainly, these types of intense but platonic same-sex friendships are nothing new. Both in the past and today they are often referred to using terms such as *romantic friendships* or *passionate friendships*. These terms are also used for those friendships in which a sexual element cannot be proven, such as the Ladies of Llangollen – Eleanor Butler (1739–1829) and Sarah Ponsonby (1755–1831) – who are persistently described as having a romantic friendship on the grounds that it is not known if they had sex. This narrow criterion downgrades all same-sex relationships to a physical one, which, of course, is not the case. It is now accepted that the Ladies of Llangollen can be considered in modern terms as a lesbian relationship.

The term *romantic friendship* was sometimes employed by same-sex couples themselves in order to divert attention. The Ladies of Llangollen deliberately cultivated the image of 'pure' platonic friendship despite the rumours of sapphism which surrounded them. The image is echoed in the fictional 'Ode to Myra' by William King (aka Frederic Scheffer) when he adds sarcastically about the lesbian character, 'Tis exalted Friendship all'. Other references include *courtly love, ritual brotherhood* or *heroic friendships* to denote various types of male bonding.

For much of history, men and women kept to separate spheres, and close emotional bonds were formed within them. When read today, letters and diaries from the seventeenth to the early twentieth centuries suggest intimacy almost like a same-sex relationship, but most were not.

Prior to the early twentieth century, many same-sex couples shared beds, and physical affection was common. Numerous photographs from the late nineteenth and early twentieth centuries show both male and female couples holding hands in intimate poses. During the period, the work of the sexologists was hidden, for the most part, denied to a general readership and often written in Latin terms to confuse lay readers. From the 1920s onwards, a flurry of marriage and sex guides, which built on the work of the sexologists, were made available to the general public. These works predominantly condemned homosexuality, the masculine woman and the effeminate man. Close physical bonds between same-sex friends began to disappear from public view.

How is it possible to differentiate between *romantic friendships, inseparable friends* or *companions, bosom friends* or *life friends* and same-sex relationships? There are common indicators which can be applied to identify same-sex relationships:

- Same-sex couples wanted to spend more time together than romantic friends did, sometimes to the point of obsession. Queen Anne (1665–1714), before she came to the throne, could hardly bear to let Sarah Churchill, Duchess of Marlborough (1660–1744), out of her sight.

- Excessive letter writing is a clue, particularly if the letters were subsequently destroyed.

- One of the familiar themes in same-sex couples is the desire to live together. While romantic friends, or the other variant terms, may express a vague desire to live together, they rarely make or carry out plans. The Ladies of Llangollen ran away together because they wanted to live together, not because they were fleeing from forced marriages, as is often claimed. Anne Lister in her diaries often refers to her practical desire to live with the woman she loved instead of simply dwelling on the idea. Many single women did live together in companionship, but without their diaries or letters it is impossible to know the true nature of the relationship.

- In the late eighteenth and early nineteenth centuries, women often lived together in 'cottage ornées', decorated or stylised 'cottages' inspired by the Romantic Movement, which represented a move away from formal, heavy architecture to a more 'natural' way of living. They were built mainly by the wealthy, even royalty, as retreats or additions to their estates. The term was coined to distinguish structures that turned a labourer's cottage into aesthetic artefact, and the cottage ornée was seen as a pure, back-to-nature way of living where children could be brought up in a heterosexual and wholesome environment. However, by the early nineteenth century, the cottage ornée was also being utilised by women living together. Designs began to reflect this, and they were being deliberately marketed as appropriate dwellings for women without families. The Ladies of Llangollen's famous house, Plas Newydd, was described as a cottage ornée, and this emphasis on female-only occupation began to undermine the heterosexual 'pure' concept. As more women moved into them, the term began to fall out of favour.

- Excessive gift giving is another indicator of same-sex couples, as opposed to romantic friendships. Whilst romantic friends did give gifts, they tended not to be as frequent as those exchanged by couples and would often be accompanied by letters explaining the significance of the gift to their relationship.
- 'Couple speak' is a good indicator of same-sex relationships. Same-sex couples describe themselves as 'we', 'our' or 'us', whereas romantic friends rarely do. Frances Power Cobbe peppered her own writings with 'our house', 'our garden', 'we' and other joint terminology about her partner Mary Lloyd: 'We gave afternoon tea to our friends under the limes ... We often had ... as many as fifty or sixty guests. In short, I had once more a home, and a most happy one; and my lonely wanderings were over.'
- Friends would write inclusively to couples. For example, letters to Frances Power Cobbe would be addressed to 'you and Miss Lloyd'. In various letters to John Gibson (1790–1866), writers asked him to pass on their 'kindest regards' to Penry Williams (1802–1885), and another asked to be remembered to Penry.
- Writings by friends should also be examined, as many individuals and couples were friends with other same-sex couples. Frances Power Cobbe and Mary Lloyd were part of a large group of friends that included Charlotte Cushman (1816–1876) and her various 'wives' as well as John Gibson and Penry Williams. Other people may have written about the couple, referred to them living or travelling together, or just gossiped about them.
- A significant inheritance left to someone who shared an individual's life may also be an indicator. While romantic friends often left bequests to each other, these rarely involved leaving an entire estate, as John Gibson did for his partner Penry Williams.
- Partners in same-sex couples may have left instructions to destroy material. For example, Mary Lloyd told her partner, Frances Power Cobbe, to destroy all of her written material. Frances did so. Posterity only has Frances's voice and silence from Mary.

Singly, the criteria cannot be used to evaluate a relationship. However, by combining several, it is easier to raise the possibility and probability that individuals were in a same-sex relationship.

Conclusion

Many people from the past are now described using modern terminology, however, because of the changing nature of certain words and phrases, this can present a false image of these individuals. For example, King Edward II (1284–1327) is often referred as a 'gay' king, most notably for his relationship with Piers Gaveston (c.1284–1312). By using the word 'gay', we run the risk of a modern audience subconsciously ascribing to him a modern gay persona, namely being exclusive to men. Yet, he had a successful and fruitful relationship with his wife, Isabella, until it was ruined by his relationship with Hugh Despenser the Younger (c.1287/9–1326). However, we cannot refer to Edward as bisexual either. The term did not exist at that time, and it would give the wrong impression to the modern reader. Probably, the most neutral way of describing Edward, Piers and Hugh, who all had relationships with women, is sexually fluid or similar.

Using modern terminology risks devaluing other relationships in the subject's life. Without proof we cannot claim the extent of love between people. Even if one speculates that Edward was probably not 'in love' with Isabella, there certainly was love there between them. How then is love valued? Whether a couple have had sexual relations cannot always be proven, and the absence of that proof cannot, as has been done in the past, be used as an excuse to erase LGBTQIA+ individuals from history. Great care needs to be taken then when describing historical people.

Researchers also need to consider that, due to the forbidden nature of certain sexual orientations, there may well be no terms used to indicate same-sex relationships. As such, we have to build up lives by examining multiple texts and presenting possible, albeit not necessarily provable, cases.

Note

1 Womanly qualities.

Bibliography

Charcot, Jean-Martin & Magnan, Valentin. (1882). 'Inversion du sense genital.' *Archives de Neurologie*, vol. 3. pp. 54–64 & 296–322.

Cobbe, Frances Power & Atkinson, Blanche. (1904). *Life of Frances Power Cobbe as Told by Herself*. London: Richard Bentley & Son. pp. 33–34.

Ellis, Havelock. (1900). *Studies in the Psychology of Sex*, Vol. 2. London: The University Press. p. 3.

Ellis, Havelock. (1928). 'Commentary by Havelock Ellis.' In Radclyffe Hall. *The Well of Loneliness*. London: Jonathan Cape. p. 3.

Freud, Sigmund. (1962). *Three Essays on the Theory of Sexuality*. Translated by James Strachey. New York: Basic Books.

James, William. (1923). 'Human Bisexuality.' *The Urologic and Cutaneous Review*, vol. 27. p. 76.

Harrison, J. H., *et al.* (1903). 'The Deterioration of Women.' *Daily Mail*. 9 September. p. 2.

Kinsey, Alfred, Pomeroy, Wardell & Martin, Clyde, (1948). *Sexual Behavior in the Human Male*. Philadelphia, PA: W.B. Saunders. p. 656.

Laurent, Emile. (1894). *Les Bisexués: Gynécomastes et Hermaphrodites*. Paris: Georges Carré. p. 211.

Lister, Anne & Whitbread, Helena, (1992). *I Know My Own Heart: The Diaries of Anne Lister, 1791–1840*. New York: New York University Press.

Marriott-Watson, H. B. (1903). 'The Deterioration of Women.' *Daily Mail*. 7 September. p. 4.

Meigs, Charles Delucena. (1867). *Obstetrics: The Science and the Art*. Philadelphia, PA: Henry C. Lea. p. 157.

Moscas de Colores. (2020). *Encyclopaedia: Gay Dictionary*. Accessed online at https://www.moscasdecolores.com/en/gay-dictionary

Moscas de Colores. (2020). *Encyclopaedia: Lesbian Dictionary*. Accessed online at https://www.moscasdecolores.com/en/lesbian-dictionary

Moscas de Colores. (2020). *Encyclopaedia: LGBT Glossary*. Accessed online at https://www.moscasdecolores.com/en/lgbt-glossary

'Population Statistics of the German Empire.' (1875). *Glasgow Herald*. 25 December. p. 3.

Scheffer, Frederick [William King]. (1732). 'An Ode to Myra.' In *The Toast, an Epic Poem in Four Books*, Book II. Translated by Peregrine O'Donald. Dublin. p. 85.

'Something for Spiritualists: A Bi-sexual Ghost.' (1894). *South Wales Daily News*. 28 May. p. 7.

Stedman, Thomas Lathrop. (1914). *A Practical Medical Dictionary*. New York: William Wood and Company. p. 466.

Stekel, Wilhelm. (1922). *Bi-Sexual Love: The Homosexual Neurosis*. Boston, MA: Richard G. Badger.

Sykes, J. B. (Ed.). (1976). *The Concise Oxford Dictionary*. 6th ed. Oxford: Oxford University Press. p. 98.

Weininger, Otto. (1907). *Sex and Character*. Translated from the 6th German edition. London: William Heinemann. p. 48.

4 Gender diversity terminology

Locating stories of gender diversity in the past can be extremely difficult. For the most part, the term 'hermaphrodite' was relied on to indicate people who would be called intersex today. Individuals we would now call trans or non-binary can be found more effectively by studying what they do, i.e., cross-dressing or cross-living, and this is reflected in the etymology of transgender terminology through the evolution of terms such as 'transvestite', 'travesti' and 'transvestism'.

Other aspects of gender diversity can be found by looking at certain biological traits, such as bearded women, at terminology incorporating gender diversity, such as 'epicene', or at stories which relied on no set terminology at all.

Rural areas are understudied for gender diversity, yet Peter Boag's *Re-dressing America's Frontier Past* (2011) and Emily Skidmore's *True Sex* (2017) show that people we would today recognise as transmen were more likely to move to rural areas than larger urban locations. More work in this area for the UK and Europe remains to be done.

Hermaphrodite

The basic definition of 'hermaphrodite' is an organism which has both female and male sexual organs. The word is taken from the Greek myth of Hermaphroditus, who was so loved by Salmacis that she prayed to the gods to allow them to be together forever. Her prayers were answered but not in the way she expected – the gods combined both their bodies into one.

The term has been used in biology since the fourteenth century. It can also be used to define something divided, such as a hermaphrodite government or a hermaphrodite brig (a ship divided into two parts).

During the nineteenth century, individual medical examinations increased, particularly for those entering the workhouse, joining the army or being sent to prison. As a consequence, scientific and medical knowledge advanced. It became apparent that the word 'hermaphrodite', when applied to animals and humans, was scientifically problematic, as the range of sexual characteristics in an individual varied greatly and could not be covered in one word. During the most active period of sexologists writing in the late nineteenth century, new definitions were applied based purely on genital existence and appearance. Terms included *true hermaphrodite* (those with both female and male sexual organs); *female pseudo hermaphrodite* (those with ovaries and male sexual organs) and *male pseudo hermaphrodite* (those with testes and female sexual organs). Another term was *psychosexual hermaphrodite*, not a person identified anatomically but someone attracted to either sexes, or an invert. As such, the term covered both sexual orientations and gender diversities.

The word 'hermaphrodite' was also used in reference to unfeminine woman or those deemed to be so by their activities, such as suffragettes, women who wore trousers or those who rode bicycles.

Some writers avoided using specific words if they were not clear about the nature of a person's anatomy, and such types of gender diversity can sometimes appear whilst searching under other terminology. For example, the following piece was found in by using the search term *gross indecency*:

1897 'Glamorgan Assizes' in the Cardiff Times

'Nauseous and disgusting'
Jeremiah Sullivan and Isaac Jones, of Maesteg, pleaded not guilty to a charge of committing gross indecency with each other ... in defence Sullivan pleaded that he was mistaken as to Jones's sex and was drunk, and Jones, that he suffered from a peculiar physical malformation, which rendered him different from other men. Prisoners were found guilty, and the learned Commissioner, in passing sentence upon them of 18 calendar months each, said the case was about as nauseous and disgusting as could be well imagined.

The definition of 'hermaphrodite' (and related terms) has gone through a range of meanings, and care needs to be taken as to which period and definition a reference comes from.

Transvestite

Magnus Hirschfeld is credited with coining the term 'transvestite' in 1910, but its French roots go back much further to the Latin *transvestire* (trans – across; vestire – clothes), which led to the French words 'travestir' and 'travesti' to denote a disguise, referring predominantly to men dressing as women:

1718 Nouveau Dictionnaire De L'Academie Françoise

TRAVESTIR. Desguiser en faisant prendre l'habit d'un autre sexe ou d'une autre condition. *On le travestit en femme pour le sauver de prison. On a travesti des soldats en paisans pour surprendre la place.*
Il s'employe ordinairement avec les pronoms personnels. *Il se travestit souvent. Se travestir pour passer au travers des ennemis.*
On dit fig. qu'*Un homme se travestit,* pour dire, qu'Il change de caractere, qu'il change sa maniere ordinarire. *C'est un scelerat qui fait le devot, il se travestit, c'est un esprit souple, facile, il se travestit, il a le don de se travestir comme il luy plaist.*
On dit figue *Travestir un Autheur,* pour dire, Faire une espece de traduction libre d'un ouvrage serieux, pour le rendre comique. *Virgile travesti.*

[TRAVESTIR. Disguising by taking the clothes of another sex or another condition. He was disguised as a woman to save him from prison. Soldiers were dressed as peasants to surprise the place.
It is usually used with personal pronouns. He disguises himself. To disguise to pass through enemies.
We say that, a man disguises himself, to say, that he changes his character, that he changes his usual manner. It is a rogue that perhaps disguises, it is a multifaceted, easy spirit, it disguises itself, it has the gift to disguise itself as it pleases.
It is said to represent an author, to say, to make a kind of free translation of a serious work, to make it comic. Virgil transvestite.]

TRAVESTISSEMENT. Substantif masculin. Deguisement. S*on travestissement ne lui a pas reussi.*

[TRAVESTISSEMENT. Male substantive transvestism. Disguise. His travesty did not succeed him.]

The word 'travesty' in literature originally meant the taking of a serious and noble subject and turning it into something ridiculous.

1775 An Universal Etymological English Dictionary *by Nathan Bailey*

Travested *travestie,* F. disguised.

Travestite *transvestitus*, L. is more especially applied to an Author, when his Sense and Stile is altered; as the Poems of *Virgil and Ovid* travestied, *i.e.* turned into Burlesque Verse.

From the 1600s *travesty* became a popular mocking literary device, and the word came into English usage following the publication of *Le Virgile Travesty en Vers Burlesques* [*Virgile Travesty*] by Paul Scarron in 1648–53. The word meant 'dressed in disguise' or dressed to appear ridiculous, and it is this association with literature and the theatre that led to the word 'travesti' denoting someone who cross-dressed on stage. In the nineteenth century it became particularly associated with women who took male roles.

Most of the *travesti* plays were light-hearted comedies, and the cross-dressing role, often central to the play, was a comic, farcical or pathetic one. The women did not attempt to disguise their voices into a lower register and, for the most part, appeared clean shaven, although a moustache may have been used occasionally. The costumes, although outwardly appearing to be male, were often feminised, thereby setting them apart from the costumes worn by men. Few *travesti* roles included playing a father, husband or man of importance. Instead, the roles usually involved the impersonation of young men. By the end of the play, the cross-dressing character would have reverted back to her 'normal' position of being unmistakably a woman.

Travesti can also be found in association with bals masqués (masquerade balls) or pleasure gardens. So prevalent was female cross-dressing at London's Vauxhall Gardens that in 1859 event organisers felt compelled to include a warning in their advertisements, such as one that appeared in in *The Era*'s 'Advertisements & Notices, that 'no Lady will be admitted in Male Attire.'

1775 The New and Complete Dictionary of the English Language *by John Ash*

Travested. Dressed so as to appear ridiculously, turn into burlesque.

Through the work being done by the sexologists in the late nineteenth to early twentieth centuries, Magnus Hirschfeld is credited with coining 'transvestism' in 1910. In these early studies of sexuality, varying theories were proposed, and a variety of terms were used to describe people, many of which are not necessarily used today. Transvestism covered people with a variety of sexual orientations or gender diversities, and Hirschfeld himself was not happy with the broad generalisation of the term. Others also rejected its use, such as Havelock Ellis, who originally replaced the word with *sexo-aesthetic inversion* but later changed it to *Eonism*. Ellis had adapted the word from the Chevalier Charles d'Eon (1728–1810), a French diplomat and adventurer who was anatomically male but gained acceptance from government and society as a woman.

Eonism was defined by Ellis:

> Many years ago, when exploring the phenomena of sexual inversion, I was puzzled by occasional cases I met with of people who took pleasure in behaving and dressing like the opposite sex and yet were not sexually inverted; that is, their sexual feelings were not directed towards persons of their own sex.

The modern term would be 'transvestite'. Now that women are free to wear clothes previously reserved for men, the term predominantly is associated with men who cross-dress intermittently. Modern definitions of eonism differ. Some retain the original negative attitude towards male cross-dressing, such as *Wiktionary* (2020), which defines 'eonism' as 'a pretence, by a man, of being a woman'. Others provide a more neutral approach, such as *dictionary.com* (2020), which defines the term as 'the adoption of feminine mannerisms, clothing, etc., by a male'.

Other modern forms of the word include 'transvestitus', most commonly used in reference to flowers and fish, such as the Nanochromis transvestitus, named as such in 1984 because the female fish is more beautiful than the male.

With the lack of specific terminology available to people in the past, other terms were used to describe those who cross-dressed or cross-lived, such as 'man-woman' and 'woman-man':

1889 The Sheffield & Rotherham Independent

> 'Kate the Rover': A Man-Woman with Two Wives.
> A woman, who gave the name of 'Kate the Rover,' and said she had been last employed in the Potteries but who appeared in male attire, was charged before the Widnes magistrates on Wednesday with wearing male clothing and being unable to give a satisfactory account of her antecedents.

The majority of results locating cross-dressing individuals can be achieved through using a variation of descriptions around *masquerading as a man/woman, pretending to be a man/woman* or *disguised as* or by using descriptions relating to dress, *in male/female attire, in male/female clothes, masquerading in male/female attire* or *disguised in men's/women's apparel*. The variety of terms available is broad. For a more complete list, see *Queering Glamorgan* (Shopland & Leeworthy 2018).

Bearded woman

Bearded women are sometimes not considered relevant to LGBTQIA+ history, as often sexual orientation or gender diversity cannot be determined in historical cases. A number of women in Barnum-type 'freak' shows were married. Spanish artist Jusepe de Ribera painted *Magdalena Ventura with Her Husband and Son* or *The Bearded Lady* (1631). Caution should be exercised when attributing a sexuality without knowledge of an individual's self-identification.

If society is expected to conform to a fundamentalist, heteronormative ideal, then anything outside of heteronormative has to be placed somewhere, particularly as bearded women were often wrongly associated with hermaphroditism.

The link between bearded women and hermaphrodites goes back to classical times, such as Aphroditus, who was an earlier version of Hermaphroditus with a female shape, clothes and a penis.

c. 400 AD Saturnalia by Macrobius

There's also a statue of Venus on Cyprus, that's bearded, shaped and dressed like a woman, with sceptre and male genitals, and they conceive her as both male and female. Aristophanes calls her *Aphroditus*, and Laevius says: Worshiping, then, the nurturing god Venus, whether she is male or female, just as the [Moon] is a nurturing goddess. In his *Atthis* Philochorus, too, states that she is the Moon and that men sacrifice to her in women's dress, women in men's, because she is held to be both male and female.

(Macrobius 2011, p. 59)

That association can be found in the twelfth century when Gerald of Wales (Giraldus Cambrensis) (c. 1146–c. 1223), in his descriptions of two bearded women, points out that one is not a hermaphrodite, whilst the other is.

1188 Topographia Hibernica by Giraldus Cambrensis

Duvenald, king of Limerick, had a woman with a beard down to her navel, and, also, a crest like a colt of a year old, which reached from the top of her neck down her backbone, and was covered with hair. The woman, this remarkable for two monstrous deformities, was, however, not an hermaphrodite, but in other respects had the parts of a woman; and she constantly attended the court, an object of ridicule as well as of wonder. The fact of her spine being covered with hair neither determined her gender to be male or female; and in wearing a long beard she followed the customs of her country, though it was unnatural in her.

Also, within our time, a woman was seen attending the court in Connaught, who partook of the nature of both sexes, and was a hermaphrodite. On the right side of her face she had a long and thick beard, which covered both sides of her lips to the middle of her chin, like a man; on the left, her lips and chin were smooth and hairless, like a woman.

(Cabrensis 1863, p. 84)

Women grow beards (naturally and not produced by deliberate and persistent shaving) due to an excess of male hormones. The causes are varied, but one of the most common is Polycystic Ovary Syndrome, a common condition that includes a high level of androgens, the compound in the body which defines male characteristics (the word 'androgen' is from the Greek *andro* meaning masculine). Numerous examples of hirsute women can be seen in historical records, and some of the earliest were perceived as supernatural or 'other', such as witches. Shakespeare utilised this tradition in *Macbeth* when Banquo speaks of the three witches.

1623 Macbeth *by Shakespeare*

Upon her skinny lips: you should be women,
And yet your beards forbid me to interpret
That you are so.
(138–46; Act 1, Scene 3, 37–45)

Very few productions of *Macbeth* include bearded witches.
Numerous bearded women can also be found in press stories of cross-living.

1847 Glasgow Herald

ENGLAND: AN AMBIGUOUS CASE – An individual, apparently about seventy, and having a long white beard, with a few days back taken up at Laon for begging, and conducted by the gendarmerie to the common place of confinement ... It was then discovered that the person taken up was a woman. For 40 years, she stated, she had worn male attire, and acted as a journeyman butcher. Her sex had never been discovered, and she would, in all probability, have gone on to the end of her career believed to be a man, had not her advanced age prevented her working as she had done formerly. Nature, in having given her a beard had suggested to her the idea of earning her bread in men's clothes in place of those of her own sex, women not obtaining employment as easily as men. The authorities ordered her to be removed to an asylum, where her wants will be provided for.

Bearded women have always fascinated society. Throughout history bearded women, for the most part, have been treated harshly and still are, including shrieking headlines, like an article by Kathy Forrester from the *Daily Mirror* (2015):

Bearded lady reveals she now loves her unshaven look after years of bullying: 'I wanted to kill myself'
A bearded woman who endured years of bullying and almost attempted suicide has spoken about her new-found body confidence.
Harnaam Kaur, 24, of Berkshire suffers from polycystic ovary syndrome and first started growing a thick facial hair at the age of just 11.
She tried to wax, bleach and shave the hair which had also started coming through on her chest and arms but finally decided to stop after being baptised as a Sikh, a religion which forbids the cutting of body hair.
Speaking during an appearance on This Morning, Harnaam said: 'At the end of the day, I love myself and the way that I'm formed.'

Since the publicity surrounding Kaur, many other bearded women have come out. The condition received further publicity from the film *The Greatest Showman* (2017). Its immensely popular theme song, 'This is Me', is sung by the bearded lady.

Epicene

'Epicene' was a word generally used as a noun encompassing both sexes. For example, 'man' or 'mankind' are epicene because they describe all of humanity regardless of gender.

1854 **A Pronouncing Dictionary of the French Language** *by B. Du Gue*

Epicene, common to both genders.

Masculine forms such as 'he', 'him' or 'his' could also be epicene, as they could be applied to women. However, in recent years there have been efforts to promote more gender-neutral terms such as 'humankind' instead of 'mankind'.

Epicene was used from the seventeenth century onwards as a synonym for hermaphrodite, androgyny or *doubtful gender*. For example, in 1682 the English priest William Richards described a cross-dressing woman in *Wallography*, his satirical work on the Welsh:

> Among rational wonders, the most remarkable Miracle of this Place was an eminent Cotquean,[1] a meer Woman in the Habit of a Man, a kind of Mal cut-purs'd Creature, an Epicene Animal of a twisted Gender, who hath a petticoat Soul in Trunk-Breech'd Body, and scandalizeth Virility by Skill in Housewifery.

A second example comes from an 1808 article entitled 'Fine Arts' in *The Examiner*, which described the paintings of Angelica Kauffman (1741–1807):

> As to the male in her pictures we should in vain look or one if he was no indicated by the masculine attire. To say the best of them, they are of the doubtful gender, of the epicene family of Hermaphroditus.

Another use of the word 'epicene' was to denote those whose gender could not be determined, such as in an 1858 article on 'Emigration' in the *North Wales Chronicle*:

> In 1857, 212,875 persons embarked at the ports of the United Kingdom in order to better their condition by removal to a more prosperous and a happier land … the emigrants included 120,279 males; 89,202 females; 3,394 emigrants appear to have been of peculiarly epicene genus, for they are marked in the registers as 'not distinguished.'

Epicene as a gender distinction does not come into use until the mid-twentieth century.

Other examples

It should be borne in mind that terminology is not always helpful, and examples can be found when searching using other keywords. The following 1802 'Tuesday's Post' article was found in the *Bury and Norwich Post* via the search term 'masculine appearance':

1802 Bury and Norwich Post

> The following curious circumstance is stated as a fact: – A servant girl who had lived with some (supposed) single *ladies* of very masculine appearance, left them some time ago, and went to live in a clergyman's family; where she had not been above a month when she was delivered of a female child. Her mistress, after repeatedly asking her whose child it was, could get no other answer than it was – '*The Lady's* where she had last lived.'

This story raises interesting questions about how we view sexual orientation and gender identity. If we accept that at least one male was cross-dressing, it can be argued that the sexual orientation could be either heterosexual or lesbian.

A useful, free publication is the *TSQ: Transgender Studies Quarterly*, published by Duke University. Its 2014 inaugural volume, edited by Paisley Currah and Susan Stryker, included 86 keywords in transgender studies and short, commissioned essays on them.

International terms

An extensive list of 'Global Terms' (2020) and a 'Glossary' (2020) can be found on the *Digital Transgender Archive* website.

Conclusion

As shown in previous chapters, set terminology can be problematic as definitions fluctuate through time. Using words and phrases, such as those associated with 'transvestite', requires great care to ensure the meaning of the original writer is conveyed rather than an impression generated by modern terminology.

Decisions also need to be taken by the researcher about what actually constitutes sexual orientation and gender diversity, such as the question of bearded women. In many cases we cannot know the sexual orientation or gender identity of these women, particularly given that in the past marriage was a must for almost everyone. Yet, the presence of a biological marker in the case of bearded women places them outside of heteronormativity.

Note

1 A coarse woman, or a man who does housework.

Bibliography

'Advertisements & Notices.' (1859). *The Era*. 13 March. p. 16.

Anon. (1718). *Nouveau Dictionnaire De L'Academie Françoise, M - Z*, Vol. 2. Paris. p. 732.

Ash, John. (1775). *The New and Complete Dictionary of the English Language*, Vol. 2. London. n.p.

Bailey, Nathan. (1775). *An Universal Etymological English Dictionary*. London. n.p.

Boag, Peter. (2011). *Re-dressing America's Frontier Past*. Berkeley, CA: University of California Press.

Cambrensis, Giraldus. ([1188] 1863). Topographia Hibernica. In Thomas Wright (Ed.). *The Historical Works of Giraldus Cambrensis*. London: H. G. Bohn. p. 84.

Currah, Paisley & Stryker Susan (Eds.). (2014). *TSQ: Transgender Studies Quarterly*, vol. 1, no. 1–2. Accessed online at https://read.dukeupress.edu/tsq/issue/1/1-2

Du Gue, B. (1854). *A Pronouncing Dictionary of the French Language*. London: Henry G. Bohn. p. 141.

Ellis, Havelock. (1936). *Studies in the Psychology of Sex*, Vol. 2. London: William Heinemann. p. 1.

'Emigration.' *North Wales Chronicle*, (1858). 2 October. p. 3.

'England: An Ambiguous Case.' (1847). *Glasgow Herald*. 15 March. p. 4.

'eonism.' (2020). *Dictionary.com*. Accessed online at https://www.dictionary.com/browse/eonism?s=t

'eonism.' (2020). *Wiktionary*. Accessed online at https://en.wiktionary.org/wiki/eonism

'Fine Arts.' (1808). *The Examiner*. 17 January. p. 45.

Forrester, Katy. (2015). 'Bearded Lady Reveals She Now Loves Her Unshaven Look After Years of Bullying: "I wanted to kill myself"' *Daily Mirror*. 17 March. Accessed online at https://www.mirror.co.uk/tv/tv-news/bearded-lady-reveals-now-loves-5348800?utm_source=linkCopy&utm_medium=social&utm_campaign=sharebar

'Glamorgan Assizes.' (1897). *Cardiff Times*. 27 November. p. 4.

'Global Terms.' (2020). *Digital Transgender Archive*. Accessed online at https://www.digitaltransgenderarchive.net/learn/terms

'Glossary.' (2020). *Digital Transgender Archive*. Accessed online at https://www.digitaltransgenderarchive.net/learn/glossary

'"Kate the Rover": A Man-Woman with Two Wives.' (1889). *Sheffield & Rotherham Independent.* 19 April. p. 3.

Macrobius. ([1542] 2011). *Saturnalia,* Vol. II: Books 3–5. Edited and translated by Robert A. Kaster. Loeb Classical Library 511. Cambridge, MA: Harvard University Press. p. 59.

Richards, William. (1682). *Wallography: Of The Britton Describ'd: Being a Pleasant Relation of a Journey into Wales.* London. n.p.

Scarron, Paul. (1648–53). *Le Virgile Travesty en Vers Burlesques.* 8 vols. Paris.

Shakespeare, William. ([1623] 1866). *The Works of Shakespeare: Macbeth.* London: George Routledge and Sons. p. 474.

Shopland, Norena & Leeworthy, Daryl. (2018) *Queering Glamorgan: A Research Guide to Sources for the Study of LGBT History.* Glamorgan Archives. Accessed online at https://glamarchives.gov.uk/wp-content/uploads/2018/08/Queering-Glamorgan-28Aug2018.pdf

Skidmore, Emily. (2017). *True Sex: The Lives of Transmen at the Turn of the Twentieth Century.* New York: New York University Press. pp. 43–67. doi:10.2307/j.ctt1pwt5nm.

'Tuesday's Post.' (1802). *Bury and Norwich Post.* 10 November. p. 2.

5 Researching in newspaper archives

Newspapers are one of the primary sources most accessed by researchers, and their use has increased greatly with the digitalisation of thousands of titles. More and more publications are being added each year. However, researchers must bear in mind that the vast array of currently available titles is by no means comprehensive. For example, most local newspapers from small towns have not been digitalised. In order to access such titles, it is usually necessary to visit a library or archive that holds original publications or microfiche versions. If multiple titles are required, it may be easier to find them all in one place in larger national archives or libraries. For example, vast collections of British newspapers are available in the British Library and the National Archives. Obviously, it is much harder to search through hard copies. *The Times* is the only UK newspaper to publish an index of its entire run. Other publications may include partial indexes. Even when indexes exist, many omitted anything that would be deemed 'unsavoury'.

This chapter looks at online newspaper archives. Some collections are accessible only through subscription, particularly those containing twentieth-century newspapers. Many publications from the nineteenth century and earlier can be accessed for free.

One of the quickest ways to uncover information, which can be done anytime and anywhere, is through a keyword(s) search. Before searching digitised sources, however, it is necessary to have an understanding of how the searching software works. Digitisation tools and software directly affect the way online newspapers can be effectively used.

Optical Character Recognition (OCR)

Optical Character Recognition (OCR) is a technology which converts an image of text into an editable and searchable form. It is widely available. Content from physical, typed sources, such as books, newspapers or archival records, can be photographed (with necessary permissions) using a camera, smart phone or tablet. The photographic image is then uploaded to an OCR conversion application, which produces a digitised text. There are plenty of free conversion apps available, such as Online OCR, SimpleOCR and Microsoft OneNote. Free apps tend to limit the amount that can be converted at a given time and require more editing of results. Paid apps, such as ABBYY FineReader, PDFelement or OmniPage, allow users to convert large or unlimited amounts of material and offer more accurate character recognition. It is important to be aware that text recognition is rarely 100 percent accurate, so some editing is necessary. While there are some technologies which can recognise and convert handwriting to digital text, such as the Intelligent Character Recognition (ICR) tools which convert handwritten notes on tablets into text, generally OCRs cannot read handwriting. Furthermore, ICR technology is still relatively new. While some free and paid apps are available, most will only recognise contemporary handwriting. Historic handwriting, particularly the more florid examples, is generally not recognised by current ICR technology.

Content from online sources accessed via a laptop or computer can be converted into images and then run through OCR software. For example, first, take a screenshot. There are a number of ways to produce an image of what is on a computer's screen:

- PrtSc button, which is in the top row on a Windows keyboard;
- Shift+Command+4 for Apple;
- *Snipping Tool* or *Snip & Sketch* in Windows or
- *Grab* in Mac.

Second, upload the image(s) to an OCR conversion app to produce searchable and editable text.

Many online search engines use OCR software to recognise typed words from scanned documents, archival records, PDF files or digitally captured images, allowing users to search for information in a multitude of languages. The software analyses the structure of text by breaking it down into lines, words and characters. It then processes the results into what it hypotheses is the most accurate version and presents it as recognisable, searchable text.

Online search engines, such as a Google search, use different technologies, often referred to as web crawlers or spiders. These may include predictive text software, which suggests alternative spellings of words, or fuzzy searches, which involve additional terms that the software deems close to the keyword(s). In contrast, OCR software is very literal. It does not do predictive text or fuzzy searches. If a word or phrase is misspelt in the OCR text, it will not appear in a search using the correctly spelled word.

OCR may also struggle to recognise certain words or characters. Damaged, ripped, faded or marked originals can cause problems. OCR can find it difficult to convert early- and mid-twentieth-century documents that were typewritten, photocopied or produced with early duplicating machines because words and characters are often quite smudged or faded. The layout and design of the page can also impact the effectiveness of OCR, which may not recognise multiple columns of type or certain typefaces.

In cases where the OCR does not accurately recognise words or phrases, it will either substitute another word or simply add what it calculates to be the correct characters. In addition, the more words used in a search phrase, the greater the chances that a character – just one character – will not be recognised, and the search will produce a 'no results' message.

When conducting research, it is important to keep in mind that what is printed in the original may not be accurately reflected in the searchable OCR. For example, a search for 'sodomy' in the National Library of Wales *Welsh Newspapers Online* database produced a false result from the *Cambria Daily Leader* in 1914 (Figure 5.1). While OCR of the article reads 'Sodomy', the word in the original was 'Society'.

It is advisable, therefore, to use a selection of possible spellings. Smudged vowels are often presented as an 'o', such as 'indecency' appearing as 'indocency'.

Words may also be split across lines, yet unhyphenated. The beginning of a word may be at the end of a textual line, while the remaining part is at the beginning of the next line. Therefore, searching for split words can produce results, i.e., 'gross indecency' may appear as 'gross ind'. Similarly, if one character in a word was not recognised by OCR, the truncated word may still be locatable through a modified search. An 1887 piece from the *Weekly Mail* was recovered by searching for

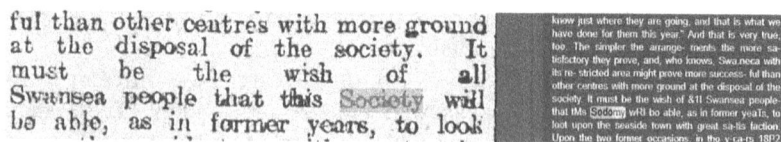

Figure 5.1 'Attendances.' (1914). *Cambria Daily Leader*. 28 May. p. 3.

'gross ind' because the letter 'e' in 'gross indecency' could not be read (Figure 5.2).

Due to the literal nature of OCR, plurals have to be searched for separately. For example, keying in the search term 'unnatural offence' into the Gale *British Library Newspapers* database yields 2,490 results, while using 'unnatural offences' yields 417. The latter term is often used as a heading under which several crimes of a similar type are grouped. Cases may appear in these groups under different headings or textual wording.

When using a search phrase, try to keep it as short as possible. The longer the phrase, the greater the chance that one character will not be recognised. If just one character is different, the whole phrase will not be recognised.

Some, but not all, online newspaper collections return OCR-based snippets on the search result page. *Trove* and *Welsh Newspapers Online*, for example, provide snippets of the textual content surrounding keyword(s). The relevance of the search results can often be instantly assessed. A great deal of time is saved by not having to open and read individual pages for each result. However, because OCR is often inaccurate in earlier publications and where content is damaged or difficult to read, the snippet may be a jumble of letters. It still may be necessary to open individual pages.

It is advisable to keep details of the articles found. Sometimes it can be difficult to relocate the pages. Rather than typing out details, using the clip tool or screen grab can save time.

John Nash, 34, and Henry Jones, 20, two soldiers, the former belonging to the Welsh and the latter to the Western Regiment, were charged with an act of gross indecency at Cardiff on the 9th of October.—Prisoners elected to give evidence on oath, and made statements in which they emphatically denied the charge, and urged that it was improbable they should have acted as described by the witnesses, assuming they had gone to the latrine for a wrongful purpose.—The jury found the prisoners not guilty, and they were forthwith discharged.

Figure 5.2 'South Wales Assizes.' (1887). *Weekly Mail.* 12 November. p. 5.

If viewing content is difficult and zoom options are not available, press the Ctrl key on the keyboard and turn the mouse wheel to enlarge the whole screen. Whenever this is done a pop-up menu will appear with the option to 'reset'. On smart tablets and phones enlarge the image by placing the thumb and forefinger on the screen and moving them apart.

Spelling

Before the late nineteenth century, spelling was not standardised. Words may be spelt in a variety of ways. For example, 'androgynous' can appear as *androgynus*, 'buggery' as *buggerie* or 'pederasty' as *paederasty*. It may be useful to use dictionaries, word books and encyclopaedias from the period being researched to check which spellings were popular for the time. Surnames and place names also may have inconsistent spellings, such as Rees/Rhys/Reece. It may be useful to make a database of name variations.

If given or family names are used to search newspaper records, bear in mind that names may be misspelt or may be aliases. Names may also be abbreviated, e.g., 'Eliz' for Elizabeth.

For multiple names or phrases, either use quotation marks around the words, i.e., "Jane Smith" or "gross indecency", or use the 'exact' option if an Advanced Search feature is available in the resource or database. It should be noted that Advanced Search tools do not always work efficiently.

Use multiple issues

While the early sixteenth century saw the first newspaper-type publications, sales were limited due to a largely illiterate population. Seventeenth- and eighteenth-century British publications are available via the Gale *Seventeenth and Eighteenth Century Burney Newspapers Collection*. The database requires an organisational login, so check local libraries and educational establishments to see if they subscribe to the archive. Some newspapers from the period are also available through the *British Newspaper Archive* (BNA), which offers subscriptions for individuals.

Newspapers grew rapidly in circulation after a series of changes from 1830 to the 1850s, including the removal of stamp duties and decreases in the cost of paper. The later part of the century saw a boom in the number of UK titles fighting for readers. As copyright was largely non-existent until around 1886, publications would often copy and paste stories sent via telegraph from a news agency. In America news syndicates supplied 'boiler plate' or 'readyprint' stories to regional publications. The former was a metal printed plate of text, and the latter were printed sheets for insertion. Editors had little or no control over the reprinting of these stories, although they would sometimes cut the plates to shorten the item to fit available space on the page. Often half of a local title would be filled with syndicated stories to the detriment of, it was often claimed, local news. Repeated use eroded and damaged the relatively soft metal boiler plate, resulting in poor copies which OCR struggles to recognise. With text from a wire service, editors could select stories they felt were of interest (or deemed suitable) for a local audience, determine which particular details to include, decide where to place it in the issue and, occasionally, add commentary, resulting in one story being presented in a variety of different ways. To interpret a story, it is necessary to access copies from a variety of publications. The selection and presentation of stories can reflect the biases of editorial staff. It would be an interesting exercise to examine which newspapers included LGBTQIA+ articles and which did not. Editors could also request certain types of stories, resulting in a proliferation of themes.

For this reason, searches should not be restricted to just a local area. Other papers, perhaps in neighbouring counties, may have reproduced the same story. County boundary lines also changed over the centuries. Since daily newspapers require more content than weekly ones, many stories are reproduced in the daily editions.

Newspapers were constantly re-edited and could produce several editions in a day, such as first, second, third, special or extra special editions. Significant local stories or content will often change from issue to issue, making it necessary to consult all versions for a comprehensive view of the story. Much of the news and information was gathered through word of mouth and rumours, however, so checks on facts via archives and others sources may be necessary.

If the OCR failed in one issue, it may well do so in others. The existence of multiple issues increased the chances of mistakes, as it meant pieces had to be reset or retyped, which made the chance of human error more likely.

Similarly, British colonial newspapers often reproduced stories 'from home'. If collections such as *Trove* (Australia) or *Papers Past* (New Zealand) are searched, it may be possible to find articles yielding names and dates, which can then be checked in British newspapers. Bear in mind that colonial newspaper databases tend to be from countries rich enough to afford digitalisation of collections.

Publications from Africa, West India and other regions and countries are poorly represented in digital resources, whether for newspapers, books, journals or other materials. Researching online is dominated by white, affluent countries. As such, collections not only reflect attitudes depicted within the content, they also reflect who primarily creates, funds or uses them.

Boolean commands and wild cards

Many internet sites, online archives and collection catalogues allow for keyword(s) searches using Boolean commands to broaden or limit the search:

- **AND** combines two or more keyword(s). Due to the fact that people may spread various terms around an article, the command narrows down the recovery of those pieces. Boolean commands do not always need to be in caps, but most search engines work better if they are. For example, putting in the words 'unnatural AND offence' will result in only those articles which contain both terms. Reversing the words, 'offence AND unnatural', will give different results.
- **OR** broadens a search. It includes any article which features the keyword(s), but not necessarily together. For example, 'unnatural OR offence' will return a huge number of hits: all articles with the word 'unnatural' and all articles with the word 'offence'.
- **NOT** excludes keyword(s) from the search. For example, the phrases *"unnatural offence" NOT child* or *"unnatural offence" NOT beast* will omit results involving paedophilia or bestiality, but only if the words 'child' or 'beast' are included in the article. On some sites, including *Google*, the – symbol (minus sign) can be substituted for NOT.

Boolean commands can be combined to produce broader results, such as *"unnatural offence" AND (male OR men) NOT (child OR animal)*. However, long search strings may return a larger number results and a high number of false hits.

Wild cards – symbols used in searches to match any possible character(s) – can also be useful:

- Adding * to a keyword will include other characters appended to the root of that word. For example, search results for *Sodom** will include sodomy, sodomise, sodomite and others.

- A possible solution to the problem of OCR mistaking one vowel for another is to use the ? to replace character(s): *sod?my*. However, it will generate false hits.
- Similarly, the ! can stand in for one or more missing characters. For example, *sapph!* will return hits for Sapphic, sapphists and others. Of course, this wild card will also return false hits.
- Wild card commands are useful for searching publications which feature the long s. Instead of an 'f', use the ? or !.

Newspapers

The first digitised archives appeared in the early 2000s. The proliferation of newspaper archive collections available online, the ongoing addition of titles and improvements in the OCR that makes them searchable means that there is a high potential for uncovering new LGBTQIA+ stories.

Newspaper collections can be accessed from home or at public venues, such as libraries and archives. *Wikipedia* provides a comprehensive 'List of Online Newspaper Archives' that includes international publications, date ranges and information about whether the archive is free or a fee-charging site.

Newspapers from 1900–2000 are not generally available for free. To access publications for this period online, it is often necessary to pay fees ranging from pay-per-view charges to yearly subscriptions. *Google News* is a free option that collates articles from around the world. It has limitations, however. Advanced search only allows up to a year. It is useful, however, for keeping informed of breaking stories.

For those wishing to research using newspapers from the nineteenth century or earlier, there are many free sites and much can be achieved without having to pay subscription fees.

Using newspaper archives is, for the most part, straightforward. There are several issues that a researcher needs to be aware of, as collections can offer very different experiences. It is worth looking through a site's 'Help' options or forums, if they exist, for hints on searching.

Where does the story sit?

There has been a traditional belief that LGBTQIA+ people migrated to large cities to take advantage of the anonymity they offered. Research by Peter Boag (2011), Alison Oram (2007) and others reveals, however, that many did not. More work needs to be done on histories of LGBTQIA+ people in rural areas and small towns. Newspaper reports of raids or arrests may indicate regular meeting places for people, such as certain pubs or clubs.

It is useful to understand the purpose, frequency, ownership, editorial stance and readership of a newspaper in order to appreciate the way an article is portrayed. As today, many historical publications were affiliated with particular groups. They reflected the political, commercial or religious views of owners, editors and the target audience. There are three guides that aid in analysing nineteenth-century newspapers:

- The *Waterloo Directory of English Newspapers and Periodicals, 1800–1900* (it operates on the 'for Wales see England' principle – Welsh newspapers are included in the 'English' directory),
- The *Waterloo Directory of Irish Newspapers and Periodicals, 1800–1900*, and
- The *Waterloo Directory of Scottish Newspapers and Periodicals, 1800–1900*.

They list publications by name and location and include details about ownership, political and religious affiliations and much more. The directories, either online or in print form, are available at some libraries and institutions. Online versions require an academic login. Some archive collections and catalogues include background information on the titles they carry. The *British Newspaper Archive* (BNA), for example, includes summaries about the papers in its collection, although some are more detailed and informative than others. The *DNCJ: Dictionary of Nineteenth-Century Journalism* (2009), edited by Laurel Brake and Marysa Demoor, provides snapshot summaries about publications, journalists, publishers and a range of subjects associated with the nineteenth-century press in Great Britain and Ireland. It is available in hard copy or via ProQuest's *C19: The Nineteenth Century Index*.

The importance of a particular newspaper story is often reflected by where it is positioned within the issue and on the page. Pages closer to the front are where the most important and most sensational stories appear. The further back in the issue, the less important the stories. Although, the length of an article may also indicate special significance.

Other articles surrounding the piece provide insight about the way the editor wanted an article to be read. For example, the search term 'unnatural offences' was often used as a heading and below it a variety of offences were listed. The tone of articles can also give an indication of how the publication viewed these types of offences. Whether an article includes differing viewpoints or takes a particular perspective may indicate if the piece was intended to inform, warn or persuade the reader.

Nearly all newspaper sites provide advanced search options, such as dates broken down into years, months and days. Awareness of when a specific word or phrase was used means the researcher can eliminate any dates when the terms would not have been in use. Further advanced searches can hone down results into counties.

Three example newspaper collections

There are numerous newspaper collections online. Search methods are fundamentally the same for most. However, sites and databases do differ in a number of ways which the researcher needs to be aware of in order to maximise returns. The three example collections – various Gale databases, *Trove* and *Welsh Newspapers Online* – and related principles that I discuss should prepare the researcher to use any other newspaper collection effectively. I do not explain every aspect of the example sites. Most are self-explanatory. The aim of the summary is to highlight methods for enhancing searches.

Gale databases

Gale, a Cengage Company which creates digital content and research tools for libraries and educational institutions, offers a wide range of databases: *British Library Newspapers; Daily Mail Historical Archive, 1896–2004; Eighteenth Century Collections Online; Gale eBooks; Mirror Historical Archive 1903–2000; NewsVault; OneFile: News; Sunday Times Historical Archive; Telegraph Historical Archive; The Illustrated London News Historical Archive, 1842–2003; The Independent Historical Archive; The Times Digital Archive* and many, many more. Subscriptions to Gale databases are only available to libraries, universities, educational institutions and similar organisations. An individual cannot subscribe. However, with a library or institutional login, they are free to access. Different institutions may subscribe to different databases. To view titles available at a particular site, access the *Change Databases* option at the top of the screen.

All resources in Gale use the same basic format, so only the *British Library Newspapers* (BLN) database will be covered here. BLN has around 160 newspapers, including national and local British newspapers, foreign newspapers, magazines and periodicals. The collection is not fully comprehensive. The majority of local newspapers are not included. There are some Welsh, Scottish and Irish publications in the collection, however. It is sometimes useful to supplement a search in Gale with searches in newspaper archives of the three countries, as they may produce different results.

Articles in Gale were created by taking images of the newspaper page (or a microfilm of the page). Copyright in the images belongs to the British Library. Reproduction of the original article (in effect, the British Library's image) is not allowed without written permission and possibly a fee.

Extracts from the content of out-of-copyright articles may be freely used. For those still in copyright, extracts are governed by the fair use laws, which determine how much can be quoted and under what circumstances quotes are allowed. For more information, see 'Fair Use Copyright Explained' (2020) on the *British Library* website.

A password is required to access BLN, which may be an academic login or your local library membership number if the library subscribes to Gale databases. Only institutions are able to subscribe to BLN.[1]

A particular newspaper can be accessed through the 'browse' option. Simply select a title from the list. A short history of the publication is included.

Entry page

The first page on a site is its entry page (or home page). The BLN entry page offers a basic search field. The 'Advanced Search' page provides the opportunity to use keyword(s), phrase combinations and topic or date filters. Unlike many other newspaper collections, BLN provides an 'allow variations' tick box, a form of 'fuzzy search' which returns imperfect matches to allow for errors or spelling variants. It is useful, but it will increase the number of false hits.

Typing a search word generates a drop-down selection list, which can provide useful alternatives. Odd aspects of this method are that the typed word does not appear on the drop-down list and the dialogue box is over sensitive. Moving the mouse to check terms or phrases in the drop-down menu may automatically change the keyword(s). Also, moving the mouse near the 'Search' option can inadvertently change the keyword(s).

Boolean commands can be selected from a menu on the left of the dialogue boxes. Types of searches can also be selected, e.g., 'Basic Search', 'Document Title', 'Entire Document', 'Publication Title', etc.

Search results

The search results page will list the article title, newspaper name and date. However, because the collection is image-driven, no snippets are supplied. It is necessary to open every page to check for relevant content. A way around this is to use the 'Topic Finder' search option.

Inputting keyword(s) returns a visualization of pertinent content that can be viewed as either tiles or as a wheel. By selecting visualisation fields, you can refine the search. For example, inputting 'sodomy' in the 'Topic Finder' narrows the search to various subjects, such as 'law', 'assizes' or 'quarter sessions' – particularly useful if researching criminal records. This method also has its oddities. For example, selecting the 'England' option will return hits from Ireland. The results are also dependent upon the quality and accuracy of the OCR running in the background, so what appears is not everything that may be related to your search.

Other search filters are available for publication date(s); article type, e.g., advertisement or news; and publication sections, such as sports or business news.

The 'Term Frequency' option is an interesting feature which shows how often keyword(s) appeared at different time periods in the publications within the collection. For example, the word 'sodomy' produces a graph from 1800 to 1900 with a spike for the year 1857. Multiple keyword(s) may be entered, allowing a comparison of terms. Obviously, results are dependent on OCR and representative only of collection publications. It is important to remember the limited nature of the dataset – hundreds of local titles are yet to be digitalised.

Another option on the search results page is the 'Broaden Your Search' button, which will search all of Gale Primary Sources for the keyword(s).

Article return page

The BLN is organised at the article level, which means the whole article is displayed when a search result is selected. However, if you want to view the whole page where an article appears, it can be selected via the 'Explore' menu. Keyword(s) are highlighted. Further options to widen the search to the entire publication are also available in the 'Explore' menu.

The option to view 'Plain Text (OCR)' is accessed via the 'Explore' menu. It can be viewed either alongside the article or separately. The text cannot be copied, but word searches within it are possible. To convert the text, use a clipping tool and run it through an online OCR converter.

Citation information can be viewed either from the 'View Full Citation' option in the left-hand menu or the 'Cite' button above the article. The 'Cite' option gives model citations based on different style manuals and facilitates the export of citation details to reference management tools and cloud storage sites.

One time-saving device in BLN is that all articles can saved, book-marked, printed or downloaded into a pdf file which is fully searchable. A text file with the article's OCR can also be downloaded. It is helpful to note that the email option sends a link to the article, not the article itself.

Translation

The only translation option available in BLN is to convert to English.

NewsVault

Gale's *NewsVault* checks 400 years of material. It primarily defaults to *British Library Newspapers*, however the orange 'Additional Resources' button will open a selection of other collections, such as the *Seventeenth and Eighteenth Century Burney Newspapers Collection* and *Independent Digital Archive*, which can be selected from a menu on the left. This feature allows the researcher to extend their search to the eighteenth century and earlier as well as access some twentieth-century collections.

Trove

Colonial papers, such as those found in *Trove* (Australia) and *Papers Past* (New Zealand), often copied stories from British and other Eng-lish-language publications. Checking these sources alongside British material is useful, as these papers were not as restricted in their lan-guage and opinions. In some cases, they were more explicit in their coverage. To locate databases with colonial and commonwealth pub-lications, consult *Wikipedia*'s 'List of Online Newspaper Archives'.

Trove is the only colonial collection considered here. It is free at the point of entry and does not require a password to search. It was one of the most user-friendly newspaper archives on the internet, however it was redesigned in 2020 and is now less so. Phrases in double quotation marks no longer return a specific phrase but return pages for each word. Even the advanced search does not allow precise searching. It is hoped these flaws will be addressed soon.

Entry page

The entry page on *Trove* allows the researcher to access a selection of archives and materials, such as books, maps, journals, digitalised newspapers and more. Entering a keyword(s) in the entry page search box will automatically access 'All categories' and all collections.

To search newspapers select 'Newspapers & Gazettes' in either the categories drop-down list within the search box or the 'Advanced Search' drop-down list just below it. The 'Newspapers & Gazettes' page has search features similar to those on other digitalised newspaper sites, such as the BLN.

Trove permits Boolean commands, but they need to be in parenthesis, such as *"unnatural offences" (men AND male)*. Wild cards do not work on the site.

Search results

The *Trove* search results page is similar to others, such as BLN. It does include snippets, so for most returns relevance can be decided at a glance. The menu on the right-hand side helpfully notes if the keyword (s) appear in the other *Trove* databases.

An extremely useful feature of *Trove* is that public users, or editors, are encouraged to tag subjects. It is a feature which should be incorporated into other newspaper archives. Even if an article includes no specific keyword(s) or terminology, a public user who believes it relates to a particular subject, such as sexual orientation or gender diversity, can tag it as such. Often, multiple tags are used to incorporate both old and new terminology. It is worth being aware that editors make spelling mistakes, particularly for 'homosexual', so try a variety of spellings when searching tags.

The tag option is extremely useful. It allows researchers to access multiple subject headings without being tied to specific terminology. Results can then be searched for and traced in British publications or elsewhere. To access public tags for keyword(s), type in the basic search box 'publictag' followed by a colon and the required word, for example, *publictag:homosexual*. When viewing an article, tags relating to the content can be found by opening the icon that resembles a luggage label in the black, left-hand menu. Clicking on any word or phrase in the list will open a new page with all articles publicly tagged with the keyword(s). Signing up for a free account allows members to add public or private tags. A 'Tags' page in the 'Become a Voluntrove' guide in the 'Help' section of the website provides more information.

Trove also offers a forum for users to discuss search methods or other topics. It also allows users to correct OCR text.

Page and article return

Trove is organised at the page level. An article's position and page number can clearly be seen, so its location within the publication can be found instantly.

The retrieved article is highlighted on the results page, while all others are greyed out. The OCR text appears on the left. The page and related content can be navigated in a number of ways. To access the greyed-out articles on the page, use the buttons just above the OCR text: the page icon ('View all articles on this page'), < symbol ('Previous article') and > symbol ('Next article'). The navigation string just above the viewing window allows you to browse articles, pages and issues as well as view information about the title.

If you click on the OCR text, the line or keyword(s) is highlighted on the page or article, which eliminates the need to search around for a particular word or phrase.

Copying text

Trove OCR text is black lettering on a white background, so it can be copied and pasted straight into a Word document. The OCR is usually of poor quality unless someone has corrected it, so copied text often requires editing. It is easy to edit the OCR text to help others, although only those who have signed up for a free membership can edit the OCR. Simply click either on the 'Edit text to match article' button on the top left or the pencil icon which appears at the end of a line when the mouse is hovered over text in the OCR field. There is even a 'Hall of Fame' for those who correct large amounts of text.

Citation examples and referencing-tool downloads are found via the 'i' button at the top of the left-hand menu.

Information about the copyright status of the material can be checked by clicking on the publication title in the navigation string at the top of the page and following the 'View title info' and 'View full title information' links.

Welsh Newspapers Online

Welsh Newspapers Online (WNO) is a free service supplied by the National Library Wales. It contains around one million pages taken from 120 English- and Welsh-language newspapers published between 1800 and around 1910. No password or registration is required for access, and it is instantly available. It is worth noting that not all publications from Wales for this period have been digitalised. The 'Media of Wales' *Wikipedia* page lists some titles not yet included in WNO.

Entry page

The WNO entry page is split into two search options. The first is a basic keyword(s) search. Searches can be limited to 'Welsh publications only' or 'English publications only' as well as by title, year and type of article, such as news, family notices, detailed lists or advertisements. The second is an option to browse and select by newspaper title, decade, region or illustration type. A useful feature is a clickable map of Wales showing the publications associated with particular areas.

Search results

After a keyword(s) search is entered the system displays either results or a message stating that no results were returned. WNO includes snippets to aid in identifying pertinent returns.

Further options to narrow the search are found via the 'Filter' menu at the top left of the results page. One of the useful features is the ability to identify copyright-free or public-domain material that can be used freely without having to check copyright status. Another useful feature is the option to split returns into decades, which is particularly helpful if you have a large number of search results to check.

The 'Advanced Search' option is straightforward and similar to most search engines. It works on the same principals as the Boolean 'AND' command. The 'Advanced Search' produces different returns than those obtained via the basic search. For example, a search for "*unnatural offence*" in WNO's basic search yields 669 results. However, an advanced search with 'unnatural' in the first box and 'offence' in the second produces 2,013 results. Due to the issue of OCR errors, this provides another option for locating articles which may have been missed elsewhere. For example, an 1842 piece from *The Welshman* concerning attempted blackmail was not found in a basic search for 'unnatural offence' because the words were too far apart, however it was recovered using the 'Advanced Search' option (Figure 5.3).[2]

to follow him, and he then turned round and said, "What the devil do you follow me for?" The prisoner thereupon turned back; but upon witness's arriving under the colonnade in Covent garden, the prisoner again came behind him and said, "If you don't, I will give you into custody upon a charge of an unnatural infamous offence?" He

Figure 5.3 'Central Criminal Court, London.' (1842). *The Welshman*. 30 September. p. 4.

Many articles used the term 'unnatural offence' to avoid shocking readers, but it was used to cover a large range of offences. It is up to the researcher to decide which results to keep, which to check and verify in other sources, such as archives, and which to discount.

Search results in WNO are ordered by relevance, with headlines listed first. Returns can appear more than once. The 'Display Options' drop-down at the top of the screen allows you to sort by relevance or date in ascending or descending order. You can also choose the number of results per page. The numbered drop-down list at the top right allows you to jump forward to a particular page of search results. To undertake a more comprehensive search, use the 'Filter' option to identify results by decade, year, month, language, region or category. The search result page also provides information about other materials in the Library's collection where the keyword(s) appear, such as journals and maps.

Page and article return

WNO is organised at the page level, which means the whole page is displayed when the search result is selected. The page is zoomable via the mouse scroll button, trackpad or the 'Zoom In', 'Zoom Out' and 'View Original Size' icons underneath the newspaper title. The technology of WNO is designed to zone in on the specific article featuring the keyword(s). It shows at a glance where the article sits on the page. The technology does not always work efficiently, however, and one can be left scanning through the whole page looking for the relevant article. It is particularly frustrating if the search term is embedded in a long article, such as 'Local News', which can run across several columns or even a whole page.

Keyword(s) are supposed to be highlighted in dark orange. Again, the technology does not always work, and one is left hunting for the reference. The issue can be circumnavigated by doing a search in the OCR text in the right-hand column. In WNO all of the text for the page appears in the OCR window, divided into separate drop-down sections for each article. Because all of the text is run together, it can be difficult at times to work out exactly where on the page the relevant text appears.

Unlike a number of other newspaper collections, WNO provides the article's page number in the information bar above the page display, which makes referencing easier. However, it has less citation information than many other sites. A *Wikipedia* citation can be accessed in the OCR window below an article's title. The site does not offer other sample citations or referencing-tool downloads. In addition, there is no facility for downloading the article or the page. Items can be saved, however, using screenshots or a snipping tool. Links for sharing items on social media are also provided in the OCR window.

Copying text

The OCR text in the right-hand column is white lettering on a black background. While the formatting makes it easier to read, it places strain on the users' eyes after several minutes.

The OCR text can be copied and pasted. If put into Word, use the 'Keep Text Only' pasting option to eliminate the appearance of white words on a black background. Another way to get around the formatting issue is to use a translation app or other online site which allows text to be pasted, then re-copy it and paste it in Word to produce a clean copy. Of course, the OCR text is rarely completely accurate, so often it will require editing.

Translating

Of course, a number of WNO articles are written in Welsh. To translate an article into English, select the OCR text, right click on the mouse or trackpad and choose the 'translate into English' option from the drop-down menu. This option does not work for tablets and phones, but holding a finger on the text for a few seconds will give a 'copy' option. The copied text can then be pasted into an online translation app. Apps that use modern languages may not be able to translate pre-twentieth-century texts. Translation apps are notoriously inefficient at the best of times, so should not be relied on too heavily. A snippet of OCR text from a 1906 *Y Cymru* article produced varying results in different translation tools (Figure 5.4).

oddiar syniad yr oes am Dduw. Yn ol yr hyn a ddywedodd Jowet, Birmingham, am duedd yr oes i wneyd Duw yn *effeminate*

Figure 5.4 'Gohebiaethau.' (1906). *Y Cymru*. 22 November. p. 6.

Collins free online translator	What Jowet, Birmingham said about the propensity of Good to do effeminate
Translate.com	What Jowet, Birmingham said about the tendency of the era to God's effeminate

The most accurate versions were produced by WNO and *Google Translate*:

WNO & Google Translate	According to what Jowet, Birmingham, said about the tendency of the age to make God effeminate

LAGNA

The Lesbian and Gay Newsmedia Archive (LAGNA) at the Bishopsgate Institute in London holds extensive press cuttings from UK national and local newspapers on all aspects of LGBTQIA+. They have an online search facility but, due to copyright restrictions, few articles are displayed. Should copies be required, it is necessary to either visit the archive or pay for copies to be sent. One very useful feature of this collection is that all cuttings have been divided into themes, such as locations or subjects, making it easier to research a specific topic.

Conclusion

There are too many online newspaper collections and databases to cover here. Some are excellent and free, such as *Trove*. Others, like *Chronicling America* hosted by the Library of Congress, can be less user-friendly. All will offer some returns if the search is as broad as possible. Skills learnt in researching newspapers, such as Boolean commands and wild cards, can be transferred to any other internet site or digitalised collection.

Notes

1 Individuals can subscribe to the *British Newspaper Archive* (BNA), a separate database product produced through a partnership between the British Library and Findmypast.
2 Finding words set apart from each other can also be achieved by using proximity operators (see Chapter 7).

Bibliography

'Attendances.' (1914). *Cambria Daily Leader.* 28 May. p. 3.

Boag, Peter. (2011). *Re-dressing America's Frontier Past*. Berkeley, CA: University of California Press.

Brake, Laurel & Demoor, Marysa. (2009). *DNCJ: Dictionary of Nineteenth-Century Journalism*. London: British Library.

'Central Criminal Court, London.' (1842). *The Welshman*. 30 September. p. 4.

'Fair Use Copyright Explained.' (2020). *British Library: Business & IP Centre*. Accessed online at https://www.bl.uk/business-and-ip-centre/articles/fair-use-copyright-explained

'Gohebiaethau.' (1906). *Y Cymru*. 22 November. p. 6.

'Media of Wales.' (2020). *Wikipedia*. Accessed online at https://en.wikipedia.org/wiki/Media_of_Wales

Oram, Alison. (2007). *Her Husband Was a Woman!: Women's Gender-Crossing in Modern British Popular Culture*. New York: Routledge.

'South Wales Assizes.' (1887). *Weekly Mail*. 12 November. p. 5.

6 Researching in genealogy, auction and social media sites

People's concepts of certain organisations and facilities tend to dominate their perception of what is possible within those services, which means areas with possible research potential are overlooked. Due to the hidden nature of sexual orientation and gender diversity history, finding new material can be hard, and any avenue that can produce results should be explored. Genealogy sites are predominantly perceived as locations for searching for families or named individuals. However, some genealogy tools allow for keyword searches, which, although not perfect, can be useful. Similarly, online auction sites are often seen as being just for the sale of goods. Yet, those very sales can provide new information. By utilising sources not generally used for research purposes, new avenues can open and additional individuals and stories can be found.

Genealogy

Genealogical websites are useful tools for fleshing out stories recovered from newspaper archives and other sources There are a lot of options. As *Family Tree Magazine* writes in its list of 'Best Genealogy Apps and Tech Tools': 'The good news: Zillions of genealogy websites exist to help you trace your family tree. The bad news: Zillions of genealogy websites exist to help you trace your family tree.' *Family Tree Magazine* summarises the '101 Best Genealogy Websites of 2020', although most of their examples are American (Fryxell 2020). Using 'best genealogical sites' in an internet search will reveal others. With such a profusion of such sites available, how does one identify LGBTQIA+ people within them, particularly when historical records can be so thin? Many genealogist records do not facilitate searches based on keyword(s), such as occupation, status, sexual orientation or gender identity.

Sites

Arguably, the most famous genealogical site is *Ancestry*. Other well-known sites include *Findmypast* and *My Heritage*. There are a growing number of free sites which offer more than just data about births, deaths and marriages. An internet search for 'free genealogy sites' will usually result in a list of international websites offering varying sources, such as obituaries, cemetery listings, newspaper articles, biographies and more. As well as general sites, there are some which specialise, such as *Find a Grave, Ellis Island, POWVETS* (WWII prisoners of war), *African Heritage Project, Jewish Gen, NativeWeb Genealogy* (Native Americans), *GenDisasters, RomanyGenes* and many more. A number of dedicated individuals provide extensive sites, such as *Cyndi's List*, which is a free site that has been available for over twenty years. The *Society of Genealogists* website provides no facilities to search keyword(s). Searching is only possible using names or places.

Names

If names are recovered in the process of researching in newspapers, archives and other sources, genealogical sites can be used to flesh out the individual's life as well as check facts. For example, the residences of writer, poet and teacher Sarah Jane Rees (1839–1916), more popularly known by her bardic name, Cranogwen, can be traced alongside that of her partner Jane Thomas. Census returns show that both women lived with their respective parents and, apparently, were not involved in heterosexual relationships. After they were freed of familial responsibilities, they moved in together.

Names taken from newspapers, criminal records or other sources often provide information which can aid in tracing an individual's movements through census records and other public documents. However, many people used aliases to avoid bringing shame on themselves and their families, therefore the lesbian and transmen named in newspaper reports often cannot be traced through genealogical records.

Keyword search

Some (but not all) genealogy sites allow keyword(s) searches. They can be used to look for individuals based on occupation, a particular address, ship names and other similar information. Keyword(s) searching is not always effective. Most sites are over helpful and inundate the search results, which requires the researcher to sift through the records. However, it is possible to use this facility on some sites to search for LGBTQIA+ keywords. For example, 'sodomy' or 'gross indecency' may bring up results from criminal or military records, extracts from newspaper reports or member blogs. Some results will be linked to partner sites. For example, a keyword search for 'hermaphrodite' in *Ancestry* produces a link to *imuseum*, an Isle of Man heritage site, which cites Ralph Cannell, the hermaphrodite child of Ralph Jnr, who died of smallpox in 1765 and was buried in the parish of Michael.

Access Genealogy, an American site that describes itself as 'the largest collection of free genealogy', will include the occasional reference. For example, a search using the keywords *in male attire* returns two cross-dressing women, and *homosexual* returns one blog on Native American Indians. A search for *sodomy* retrieves a pertinent article on 'The Osage of Kansas' (2020):

> Sodomy is a crime not uncommonly committed; many of the subjects of it are publicly known, and do not appear to be despised, or to excite disgust; one of them was pointed out to us; he had submitted himself to it, in consequence of a vow he had made to his mystic medicine, which obliged him to change his dress for that of a squaw, to do their work, and to permit his hair to grow.

We Relate is a *Wikipedia* project. Rather than compiling its own listings, it encourages users to upload their own. Searches for some terms simply result in links to Wiki pages. Others produce personal listings or blogs on various subjects, which can contain nuggets of information, such as the story of William Jones, who in 1763 was accused of buggery, and the story of Clarence Aldor Gauthier, whose wife was 'a lesbian, "kinda gay girl"'.

GENUKI: UK and Ireland Genealogy is one of the oldest genealogy sites. It is a non-commercial venture run by volunteers and provides links to genealogical sites throughout the UK. Keyword(s) searches will pick up bits and pieces. For example, a search in 'Indictable Offenses (c.1745 – c.1782)' identified John Kallendar, a labourer of West Teignmouth, Devon, who was charged with assaulting Richard Sarell with an 'intent to commit that most horrid detestable and Sodomitical Crime called Buggary' (Brassett 2020).

Publications

Genealogy sites often include a variety of publications, such as newspapers, and keyword(s) searches will return results from these materials. *Findmypast* has four searchable collections: *British Newspapers,*

Irish Newspapers, PERSI (PERiodical Source Index) and *US and World Newspapers*. It is a paid site, but paying for a genealogical site that includes newspaper searches may be more cost effective than paying for a newspaper site subscription. Compare and contrast prices to find the cheapest option.

Auction sites

Auction sites may not immediately come to mind as resources for researching LGBTQIA+ history, however useful information can be found. As with almost everything, there is a *Wikipedia* page covering 'Online Auction Websites', but it is not fully comprehensive. Better results can be found by doing an internet search for 'best online auction sites' or similar. Familiar names will appear, such as *eBay, Etsy, eBid, Delcampe* and others.

Research tips on auction and sales sites often include advice to include words commonly misspelt, such as 'lesbain' instead of 'lesbian'. Trying alternative spellings can reveal items bypassed by those who only use correct spellings, and bargains can be acquired. However, with the widespread use of free grammar checking apps, bargains based on misspelt words are harder to find – but it is still worth trying.

Often auction site keyword(s) searches only return hits based on terms included by the vendor in the metadata. To ensure that item descriptions are also searched, look for additional search options, such as 'include description' or 'title and description' tick boxes provided on some sites.

Boolean commands have some use. Unfortunately, however, searching is blighted by the marketing ploy of tagging anything and everything possible as 'gay interest' – even a pink coloured washing line may be tagged 'gay interest'.

Examples included here are predominantly from *eBay*, as it produced the best results. Given the rapid turnover of items on auction sites, however, items of interest can appear elsewhere.

Books, CDs and videos

If books, CDs or videos listed on auction sites include keyword(s) terms within their metadata, they can give a useful indication of LGBTQIA+ titles that are available. This will only work, however, if a keyword term is included. Quite often vendors simply copy and paste the title, author/artist, production details and any blurbs that are available for the items they post for sale. This means that works which do not contain LGBTQIA+ details in their listings will not show up in keyword(s) searches. For example, the archaeological works of Jane Dieulafoy (1851–1916), the highly regarded French archaeologist, are widely available on auction sites. However, a copy of her novel *Volontaire* (1892), which is considered by Rachel Mesch (2017) and others to be one of the earliest trans novels, appeared on *eBay* in 2020 for €130. It was not tagged as such, and it had no buyers.

Films which are rarely shown on commercial channels can also be purchased on auction sites and used by social groups or during celebratory events, such as LGBT History Month and Pride. If a film is to be shown in public, such as at an event, the venue will need a film licence. Most local libraries, archives, museums and the like will have the necessary licensing.

Ephemera

Short-life items often appear on auction sites, such as bar cards, calendars, cartoons, e-flyers, event posters, film posters, handbills, phone cards, political badges (which have become very collectable in recent years), political paraphernalia and the like. LGBTQIA+ venues or events which have disappeared may still be represented by bar cards, fliers, posters or similar. Searches using the Boolean command 'gay AND poster' or searches for 'beer mat', 'coasters', 'flyer' or the like will produce results in those categories. Or, search for a known location, such as a pub name. Click on the 'used' option to view vintage items rather than new or reproduction merchandise.

Crime is well represented in ephemera. A search for 'sodomy' in *eBay*'s 'Collectables' marketplace results in various FBI wanted posters from the 1960s and 1970s and wire press photos of individuals arrested on sodomy charges.

Vintage magazines can also be purchased on auction sites, particularly back copies from publications dedicated to LGBTQIA+ matters, which are commonly referred to as the 'Pink Press'. A 'List of LGBT Periodicals' is available on *Wikipedia*.

Collecting ephemera is useful to build up collections for exhibitions or displays.

Letters

In 2017 Mark Hignett, curator at Oswestry Museum, was searching for items relating to the town when he came across some letters for sale on *eBay*. After purchasing a few he realised the correspondents were writing love letters to each other. Mark acquired the rest of the collection. It was only after he had gone through them and put the story together that he realised the correspondents were two male soldiers. The story went viral. *Pink News* published a piece on it in February 2017. There are rumours of a film being made, and the letters are now on display at the museum. Hignett's experience is a rare occurrence, but it proves that the acquisition of letters or other materials on auction sites can recover information about LGBTQIA+ individuals.

Letters or contracts from named celebrities or well-known people can also be found on auction sites.

Miscellaneous auction items

Various other merchandise items are available on auction sites, including vintage t-shirts, which often feature political messages, funny slogans and similar. Some are hand-made, but most are mass-produced. They can be interesting additions to exhibitions and displays.

For miscellaneous items, it is worth checking the 'everything else' category in *eBay*.

Photos

After the invention of the daguerreotype in 1839, portraits became important tools for preserving images of celebrities, family members and loved ones. In the nineteenth century, there was a fad for collecting cartes de visite, photographic images of royalty and famous individuals mounted on card. The early twentieth century saw a proliferation of images of same-sex couples in close affectionate poses. These died out, however, once the public became more aware of homosexuality. After WWII they tend to disappear. Some vendors either mistake these images as representations of homosexuality or deliberately use LGBTQIA+ tags as a marketing ploy, although some, indeed, may be of same-sex couples. The keyword 'lesbian' results in a large selection of soft porn photos, both old and modern. The term 'cross-dressing' is more useful and returns images of gender diversity.

Other vendors do, however, undertake research, and they tag known LGBTQIA+ people. At the time of writing, *eBay* advertised an 1870s photograph of Lucy Tait (1841–1918), the lover of Mary Benson (1856–1938), for £65. I have used auction sites to buy photographic images of Frances Power Cobbe (1822–1904), Harriet Hosmer (1830–1908) and others.

Postcards

The first commercial postcard appeared in the United States in 1861. By the late nineteenth century, they were being mass produced. Before the telephone became widely available, postcards often facilitated virtual conversations due to the speed of post office delivery. These exchanges can provide interesting social commentary. Check the backs of postcards purchased through auction sites. They may reveal a relationship between the written and visual messages. Pay attention, for example, to women who sent postcards to women from places like Plas Newydd, the home of the Ladies of Llangollen. Or, if men sent postcard portraits of individuals, such as Oscar Wilde, to men, then pay attention to whether the message contains any cynical or romantic comments.

For named individuals, portrait postcards and cartes de visite can be acquired. If out of copyright, they can be freely used for illustration purposes, although check to ensure that the card is not a reproduction, as these may be covered by copyright.

Vendors will often tag postcards that depict two women or two men together as 'gay themed', 'gay interest', 'lesbian' or similar, despite there being no evidence to support this tagging. Terms are sometimes accompanied by a question mark. Soft porn images of women together are often tagged as 'lesbian'.

Miscellaneous

The internet is awash with social media sites: *Facebook, Twitter, Tumblr, Instagram, WhatsApp, Skype, Snapchat, Pinterest, LinkedIn, YouTube* and others. There are also many less well-known and non-English-language sites. New sites are continually popping up.

Many of these platforms include societies, groups, forums and the like, which specialise in almost every possible subject and can be either local or international. LGBTQIA+ venues use social media to promote events. By joining the pages of local heritage organisations or groups, members can be kept aware of any events taking place, such as history months or celebratory days. For example, the London Metropolitan Archives has a dedicated *Facebook* page, 'LGBT History at the London Metropolitan Archives', which can be found by searching for '@lgbthistory'. Many organisations will not allow direct posting to their social media pages. However, it is often possible to share and comment on posts.

Numerous 'calls for papers' for conferences or publications appear on social media, which can illustrate current research trends or identify regular conference hosts and organisers.

Many forums also exist outside of social media. Genealogical sites, for example, often include internal forums.

There are hundreds of social media groups specialising in history, including ones dedicated to local histories or specific subjects. Posting on these sites or joining their mailing lists provides opportunities to share research, raise visibility and fight discrimination. Often in these discussions, members will post references or information, including personal stories. The stability of these sites can be tenuous. While a member can save an individual post, only a site administrator can retain the group site. If the site is deleted, the information is lost.

'WikiProject LGBT Studies' is free to join for anyone with a *Wikipedia* account. Its aim is to improve coverage of LGBTQIA+ content on *Wikipedia*.

Rictor Norton's *Gay History and Literature* (2019) website also has many useful links.

Mailing lists

Mailing lists are useful for keeping abreast of current research, calls for papers, events and so on as well as for networking or posting requests for information. Universities often have dedicated LGBTQIA+ mailing lists to keep students updated on all events, local venues and general information. Wikimedia has a free mailing list intended to facilitate discussions of strategies and approaches for increasing LGBTQIA+ participation in Wikimedia projects. *JiscMail*, a platform for 'email discussion lists for the UK Education and Research communities', is a particularly useful academic mailing list service. Membership is free. There are a number of LGBTQIA+ lists, such as ANTEQUEERIANS, LGBTQ-HISTORY, LGBTQ-MUSIC, QUEERMUSEUMSNET-WORK, QUEERSCREENS and others. Members subscribed to a particular list receive emails containing requests for information, calls for papers, notices of events and similar. Members can also submit pertinent posts. Individuals and groups can start their own mailing lists if they fit JiscMail's eligibility criteria.

Elsewhere numerous organisations, social media groups, blog writers and others provide mailing lists. It is just a case of searching for and finding those most relevant to the individual researcher.

Conclusion

The types of internet sites listed above can aid in researching modern or past histories and help flesh out exhibitions or displays.

LGBTQIA+ research is as much about finding new people and information as it is about fleshing out details on known histories and people. Existing tools have shortcomings. Genealogy sites need to look at improving ways of finding information based on keyword(s) searches, such as blindness, deafness, physical disability, race, religion, sexual orientation, gender diversity and other characteristics. One option would be to allow site users to tag content, as is possible on other sites such *Trove*, a freely accessible digitised collection of materials from Australian libraries, universities and cultural institutions. Tagging facilitates research enormously.

Official institutions, such as archives and museums, may be unable to purchase LGBTQIA+ items on auction sites due to the lack of provenance evidence. However, individuals can build up collections, often very cheaply, which can be loaned or donated to heritage organisations. I built up my own large collection of books, documents, artefacts and ephemera related to Welsh LGBTQIA+ heritage mainly from auction sites and mainly at reasonable prices.

Bibliography

'Best Genealogy Apps and Tech Tools.' (n.d.). *Family Tree Magazine*. Accessed online at https://stevemorse.org/101best/101best2018.html?cat=Tools

Brassett, Brian. (2020). 'Indictable Offences (c.1745 – c.1782): Devon Quarter Sessions, DRO – Devon QS10/1.' *GENUKI: UK and Ireland Genealogy*. Accessed online at https://www.genuki.org.uk/big/eng/DEV/CourtRecords/QS10-1

Dieulafoy, Jane. (1892). *Volontaire*. Paris: Colin.

Fryxell, David A. (2020). '101 Best Genealogy Websites of 2020.' *Family Tree*. Accessed online at https://www.familytreemagazine.com/best-genealogy-websites

'List of LGBT Periodicals.' (2020). *Wikipedia*. Accessed online at https://en.wikipedia.org/wiki/List_of_LGBT_periodicals

Mesch, Rachel. (2017). '"O My Hero! O My Comrade in Arms! O My Fiancée!": Gender Crossing and Republican Values in Jane Dieulafoy's Fictions.' *PMLA*, vol. 132, no 2. pp. 314–330. doi:10.1632/pmla.2017.132.2.314.

Norton, Rictor. (2019). *Gay History & Literature: Essays by Rictor Norton*. Accessed online at http://rictornorton.co.uk

'Online Auction Websites.' (2020). *Wikipedia*. Accessed online at https://en.wikipedia.org/wiki/Category:Online_auction_websites

'Read These Love Letters from a WW2 Soldier to his Boyfriend.' (2017). *Pink News*. 17 February. Accessed online at https://www.pinknews.co.uk/2017/02/17/read-these-love-letters-from-a-ww2-soldier-to-his-boyfriend

'The Osage of Kansas.' (2020). *Access Genealogy*. Accessed online at https://accessgenealogy.com/kansas/the-osage-of-kansas.htm

'WikiProject LGBT Studies.' (2020). *Wikipedia*. Accessed online at https://en.wikipedia.org/wiki/Wikipedia:WikiProject_LGBT_studies

7 Researching in libraries, books and journals

Opportunities for uncovering material on the internet are vast. With the sheer scale of constantly-changing information, the difficulty is finding it! In the last few decades the number of books, journals and grey literature available on the internet has exploded. This chapter looks at ways of researching in such a challenging environment.

Finding written content

Locating written content in whatever medium often begins with a general internet search. Results can be increased and improved through the use of variant commands or operators. Chapter 5 included information on Boolean commands and wild cards, which can also be used in general internet searches. Proximity operators are additional, helpful tools for finding results where search terms are in close proximity with, but not next to, each other.

- **NEAR**, which uses the shortcut 'N/#', finds search terms (in any order) separated by a certain number of words. The default distance is four words either before or after. Greater or smaller intervals can be specified by placing a backslash and a number after the 'N', with the maximum being 255. For example, '*lesbian NEAR/3 London*' will return material with the word 'lesbian' three words apart from – either before or after – the word 'London'. The NEAR proximity operator differs from the AND Boolean operator, which returns keyword(s) from an entire document.
- **WITHIN**, indicated using 'W/#', does the same thing as **NEAR** when a number designation is used, but this operator returns only instances where the words appear in the order entered.
- **NOT NEAR** or **FAR** places a keyword(s) a designated distance away from another term. For example, searching for 'Wales'

always returns hits for 'England and Wales' and 'New South Wales'. In principal, this command should distance keyword(s) such as 'England' or 'New'. However, it does not work well. The Boolean command **NOT** works better.

Other proximity operators include FOLLOWED BY, NOT FOLLOWED BY, SENTENCE, PRE, EXACT and AROUND. Researchers can experiment to identify those operators that work best for a particular subject area.

The 'less than' (<) and 'greater than' (>) symbols are sometimes suggested as tools for narrowing searches for dates or numbers, however they make no significant changes to results in a general search.

Boolean and proximity operators can be combined in a variety of ways to suit the researcher. The greater number of tools utilised will result in a greater number of returns.

Finding books on the internet

For researchers, access to books is vital, but locating LGBTQIA+ titles or content on the internet is not always a straightforward matter.

In the last few decades, the publication of books on sexual orientation and gender identity has risen. Increases are partly due to the opportunity to self-publish on a variety of platforms as well as publishers accepting and offering print-on-demand manuscripts. Some new titles can be found by searching for terms, such as 'best LGBTQIA+ books', to produce a variety of results, which are often reading lists assembled by organisations to mark celebratory events, such as Pride. For example, the Penguin Random House website includes '*The Ultimate LGBTQIA+ Pride Book List*', *Amazon*'s Books department has a 'Lesbian, Gay, Bisexual & Transgender Books' section and *Harper's Bazaar* publishes an annual 'Best LGBTQ+ Books' list.

A variety of book apps, online bookstores and similar sites provide alerts and notifications of new works by author(s) or subject(s) so registered members can conveniently stay up-to-date on new releases.

Bookshops

Wikipedia has a 'List of LGBT Bookstores', which includes dedicated shops and stores containing themed sections. The two most well-known shops in the UK are *Gay's the Word Bookshop* in London, which was founded in 1979, and *Category is Books* in Glasgow, which opened in 2018. While large, general bookshops possibly have themed sections, most small shops do not. Content in general bookshops is usually celebrity-driven or general titles.

Bookshops often have options for purchasing online, or orders can be placed through online-only stores, such as *Wordery*.

Libraries

National libraries

The British Library is the world's largest library. It contains not just books but a huge variety of publications, non-print media and archives of interest to the LGBTQIA+ researcher. For example, the Hall-Carpenter Oral History Archive, part of the National Sound Archive, focuses on the gay and lesbian experience in Britain. Most keyword(s) searches in the Main Catalogue have numerous results. There is a dedicated 'LGBTQ Histories' page on the website featuring blogs and items from the collections.

The catalogues of Leabharlann Nàiseanta na h-Alba – the National Library of Scotland and Llyfrgell Genedlaethol Cymru – the National Library Wales return good results for most keyword(s) searches, allowing a review of what publications exist.

Leabharlann Náisiúnta na hÉireann – the National Library of Ireland, which incorporates Northern Ireland, produces results mainly related to modern terms. The website tends to return the same set of results.

Public libraries

The stocking of LGBTQIA+ titles in public libraries across the world has long been – and continues to be – a contentious topic. However, the debate is outside the scope of this book. Early classifications and cross-referencing reflect discriminatory attitudes of the times when they were created. For example, some books were cross-referenced to 'sexual perversions'. A number of task forces were set up to address the issue of bias in classification, particularly in the US. In 1986 the American Library Association established a Task Force on Gay Liberation to address the sexist and homophobic labelling which had prevailed in classifications. As a result, an *International Thesaurus of Gay and Lesbian Index Terms* was published in 1988, although it is now extremely difficult to acquire or consult (Gregg & Rindinger 1988). However, Matt Johnson's '*GLBT* Controlled Vocabularies and Classification Schemes' (2007) is available online. In addition, a number of groups were set up in the UK to look at LGBTQIA+ issues and libraries, including the Gay Librarians Group (1973–1979), the Lesbian & Gay Librarians Group (1985–1990) and the Burning Issues Group (1994–2000). Most recently, the Chartered Institute of Library and Information Professionals (CILIP) established the LGBTQ+ Network, which was just being organised at the time of writing.

Despite campaigning in various countries, many libraries still do not keep large selections of LGBTQIA+ books. In some places, due to external pressures, libraries have been removing books from their shelves, particularly those for young people. However, the majority of UK public libraries purchase and display LGBTQIA+ books and other materials. The Surrey County Council's Libraries website includes an 'Out Lit' collection of books. Southampton City Council provides a page of 'LGBT Reading Lists'. Tameside Metropolitan Borough Libraries offers a webpage with 'Services for Lesbian, Gay, Bisexual and Transgender People (LGBT)' and identifies its LGBT book collections with a rainbow triangle on the shelves and books' spines. Some users may feel uncomfortable, however, publicly taking out and reading something which so openly declares their interests.

Public libraries can be located through *GOV.UK* or individual council websites. Library locations are identified by entering a postcode. Most libraries have an OPAC (online public access catalogue) which can be used to search for titles or topics. Alternatively, online databases of catalogue information from multiple institutions, such as *WorldCat*, can be used to conduct international library searches via book title or keyword(s). Entering a postcode in *WorldCat* will reveal nearby location(s) where resources are held. While *WorldCat* is fairly comprehensive, it is restricted to those libraries which have signed up to the organisation.

Public libraries in towns or cities will generally carry more stock than rural libraries. Most allow membership for those living or working in the area. Joining several libraries allows the researcher greater access to different resources.

Members of public libraries may request inter-library loans of many books published in the UK. If a book is acquired from another library within the same library service, the process is usually straightforward and free. If the loan is from a different library system, costs may be incurred, which vary according to the level of charges set by the local authority. Increasingly, unfortunately, more costly books, such as academic titles, are not available through inter-library loan because no public library service has purchased a copy.

Dedicated libraries or collections

There are few libraries, or collections within libraries, dedicated to sexual orientation and gender identity. Where they do exist, they tend to be in major cities, such as the London Metropolitan Archives, the British Library or the libraries in Liverpool and Manchester.

The University of Reading's 'LGBT+ Library Resources: Other Libraries and Archives' (2020) page provides a useful list of 22 international organisations, including 13 in the UK and others in the United States, Canada and South Africa. It is not an exhaustive, however, The list omits, for example, the Schwules Museum (Gay Museum) in Berlin and the IHLIA LGBT Heritage in Amsterdam.

There are dedicated libraries and collections in the UK. The National Library of Scotland aims to collect all Scottish, UK and significant non-UK published material. *The Lesbian Archive* at Glasgow Women's Library is home to one of the most significant LGBTQIA+ historical collections in the UK. LAGNA at the Bishopsgate Institute holds a large, general library, as does the Hall Carpenter Archive at the LSE Library in London. Individuals may also amass significant collections. For example, I hold an extensive, private collection of Welsh LGBTQIA+ books.

The high price of academic and textbook titles has long been a sticking point for many researchers and libraries. A possible alternative to purchasing is renting titles. Search for 'textbook rental sites' to identify rental schemes. Some post hard copies, others provide digital copies which expire on a particular due date. Publishers, such as Routledge, also provide digital rentals on many titles for a fixed term. Check the book's original publisher to see if rental is possible.

University libraries

Some universities hold collections which the public can access on a daily basis via a reader's ticket. In many instances, books must be consulted on site. Taking books out on loan often involves a yearly subscription. For example, Cardiff University offers the CLIC (Cardiff: Libraries in Cooperation) scheme for members of the general public. Individuals living, working and studying in Cardiff can pay £10 a year to take books out on loan from Cardiff University, while anyone living outside the city pays £60 a year. Other universities have much higher fees. Leeds University, for example, charges a member of the public between £100–£200 annually. Many other institutions only provide details about public access upon application.

Online publications

The amount of data available online can be overwhelming. Putting well-known terms into an internet search, such as 'tribade', will generate over 800,000 results. While the most relevant should appear at the beginning of the list, there is still the danger that some material will remain undiscovered. There is also the risk that many hits are the result of misspellings or OCR misreadings, so it is advisable to redefine the search. By utilising Boolean commands or wild cards the search can be altered. For example, a search for 'tribade AND woman' still produces over 100,000 hits, but returns interesting top results. Further experimentation can be done by changing 'woman' to 'women' or adding 'lesbian' to generate a different set of results. Further refining can be done by using other options within the particular search engine, such as 'books' or 'magazine'. Searching online for books is valuable. Much of the pre-1923 material available online is free to download and copyright free, which means it can be widely disseminated.

With such a huge amount of material now available, there is so much to discover. The glossary in *Queering Glamorgan* came about due to research into female same-sex and gender diversity in history. Over 3,000 items have been recovered so far. The majority of what has been found remains unpublished outside the original source, including books serialised in newspapers. In fact, many books written for serialisation have never been reprinted.

There are numerous sites offering public domain digital libraries, although much of the content is replicated either as identical copies or different versions. The advantage of multiple copies is the opportunity to compare material for changes which may reflect societal or legal conditions.

Some editions, such as Kindle, EPUB and others, do not contain page numbers, which poses a consistent problem for researchers when it comes to citing references. To get around the lack of page numbers, check if a paginated copy of the publication is available elsewhere.

Three online digital libraries will be examined here: Google Books, Internet Archive and Project Gutenberg. All are free, require no logins and offer search mechanisms that are similar to other collections. Some content is out of copyright and free to use, however it is still possible that materials are subject to copyright. In addition, freedom of use may not be applicable in some countries due to their copyright laws, so copyright issues need to be checked.

Google Books

Google Books does not have a dedicated website. Inputting the name will take the user to a book search page on Google itself. The search box allows keyword(s) searches of all publications available in Google collections. According to *Wikipedia*, 25 million scanned books had been uploaded by partnered projects as of 2015.

Google Books is free to use, requires no login, and has four access levels:

- *full view* – publications in the public domain that are free to view and download.
- *preview* – works currently in print and protected by copyright. Copying and downloading are prohibited, but a portion of the book is available to view. Google Books sets a minimum of 20 percent viewable content, but the publisher can elect to increase the amount that can be previewed.
- *snippet view* – just a handful of lines from the book are shown because Google does not have copyright permission to display any more content.
- *no preview* – books which have not been digitalised but exist elsewhere.

The last two options can be helpful even though they provide little or no view of the content, because they suggest publications are available in some form somewhere.

The 'Any time' drop-down menu on the search results page allows you to narrow a search by century or a customised date range. It is a useful way to identify nineteenth-century or early-twentieth-century works. For example, books by sexologists from this period are often freely available via Google Books and other sites.

Opening a hit in Google Books provides a result page that includes a search box on the left. It can be used to locate content within the book. If searches consistently return no hits, try a common word, such as 'and', just to see if the OCR is working. To download a free book, click on the sprocket wheel icon at the top right above the reading window and choose 'Download EPUB' or 'Download PDF'. Clicking on the 'Ebook – Free' button on the top left will take you to the *Google Play* platform where books can be also be downloaded, read and saved.

If you require just a page or paragraph, rather than a full download of the book, click on the sprocket wheel icon and select 'Plain text', which reveals the OCR version of the book. To locate the passage you want to copy in the plain text, use the Windows 'Ctrl + f' or Apple 'Command + f' shortcut to find a keyword(s).

If a copy of a small amount of the original text is required, take a screenshot or use the Windows *Snipping Tool* or *Snip & Sketch*, which are useful applications that can be found on the computer's list of programs or searched for by name. After opening the tool, select 'New' and click and drag around the area required for copying. Copies can then be immediately pasted into another document or saved as an image. The tool also allows users to highlight or write over the copied material, so notes can be made directly on the image.

If the content recovered requires translating, there are a number of options:

- For public domain publications, access the sprocket wheel icon and select the 'Plain text' option. A menu will appear offering to translate the text if it is in a language other than the computer's default language.
- Alternatively, once a book has been opened, select the scissor icon on the bar above the text and highlight a portion of text. A 'Share this clip' pop-up window will then appear. Clicking on 'Translate' will open a new Google Translate window with the selected OCR plain text alongside a translation in a language selected from the menu. As with any OCR text conversion, the results often include multiple errors, and hard-to-read originals will result in greater mistakes. In addition, translation apps are not perfect, particularly for historic material. The resulting text is also presented in a continuous stream, which does not reflect the formatting in the original document and makes it necessary to break it up for reading. Google Books will always default to Google Translate, but other translation apps are available.

All books on Google can be added to a personal library through the 'My library' option on the sprocket wheel icon menu. This is particularly useful. As there are so many little-known LGBTQIA+ works, publishing the 'My Library' list may raise awareness of these works and make them easier for others to find.

Some public-domain books digitalised by Google are not free to download because Google has copyrighted the scanned images and sells the books through online outlets. These are simply the OCR text in print form with uncorrected errors. The original texts are still public domain and, therefore, free to use. However, without the original to compare to, it can be difficult to create an accurate text using the OCR version. Before buying one of these scanned books, always see if it is available elsewhere.

Internet Archive

Internet Archive is a digital library based in America that is free to use and requires no login. It is one of the world's largest book digitalisation projects, scanning about 1,000 books a day. The project began in 1996 as a repository of web pages, something not generally collected or covered elsewhere. The website now has millions of pages of books, films, TV, music, journals, websites and more.

Internet Archive includes books that are not in the public domain. Once registered as a free member, users can take out books on a time-restricted basis through its *Open Library* site.

The entry page allows five basic search options: 'Search metadata', 'Search text contents', 'Search TV news captions', 'Search radio transcripts' and 'Search archived websites'. Modern terms work well in all five categories. An advanced search option allows Boolean commands, but wild cards will not work. Using quotation marks around a phrase works well. Search results can be refined using a variety of options, including date ranges.

Metadata usually only includes what the book is about and the main topics covered, so 'Search text contents' often offers more returns.

The book will open on the page identified through the search. A position bar at the bottom and a blue marker identify exactly where in the book the search term(s) are located. A number of download formats are provided as well as full citation details. For foreign-language books, select 'full text', copy the relevant text and paste it into any translation app.

One difficulty with Internet Archive searching is what appears when the text is opened. While a full search term in inverted commas may be used to locate information in the first instance, when the book is opened the relevant page often fails to load. The user is left on the first page and, because the search results do not include page numbers, it can be difficult to locate the item or relevant text. If you reduce the search phrase to one word, the search invariably works.

Project Gutenberg

Project Gutenberg was the first initiative to digitise books in 1971. Perhaps fittingly, the first e-book was the *Declaration of Independence of the United States of America.* Unlike Google Books, Project Gutenberg only offers material in the public domain. Its catalogue has around 60,000 titles. Around 50 titles are uploaded each week. Many of the books sold as OCR versions on Google and other sites are free on Project Gutenberg.

Books on the site are available in a variety of formats that are compatible with most platforms, such as Kindle, HTML, PDF, EPUB, Mobi, Plucker and plain text.

Due to the highly unreliable nature of OCR text, Project Gutenberg associates with *Distributed Proofreaders*, an online group of volunteers who correct material to make volumes as accurate as possible. This freedom of information has caused controversy. Work done by volunteers means others can – and do – reproduce and sell the books commercially. The *sweat of the brow* doctrine means no amount of labour devoted to perfecting public domain works can produce a new copyright in the work.

Project Gutenberg does have a category section which catalogues books into popular subjects, such as animals, music and religion. No LGBTQIA+ categories are included.

The site is free to use and requires no login. Essentially, there are only two search options: a book title search under 'Browse catalogue' and a keyword(s) search under 'Book search'.

When putting in keyword(s) it should be borne in mind that public domain material, especially if originating in the USA, only includes titles prior to 1923. Therefore, better results will be generated if you search for terms commonly used prior to this date. For example, the word 'homosexual' was just being established at this time, so using it for a basic search will only result in a small number of hits. Many sexual orientation terms, such as 'sodomy', 'buggery', 'tribade' and 'sapphism', return no hits. No works reflecting these terms seem to have been included or tagged. Therefore, it is necessary to use terminology outside the modern, standard terms. Try using variations around cross-dressing and cross-living, for example. A detailed list can be found in *Queering Glamorgan* (Shopland & Leeworthy 2018).

Using quotation marks to restrict searching to an exact phrase does not work effectively in Project Gutenberg. With patience results can be obtained. For example, the phrase "*dressed as a man*" returns 31 hits, but many do not contain the terms. Even the word 'dressed' is not included in some. However, by persistently checking every hit, results can be found, such as the item 'A Notorious Female Doctor' from *The Funny Side of Physic* (1874) by Addison Darre Crabtree (Figure 7.1).

A NOTORIOUS FEMALE DOCTOR.

WASHINGTON, January 10, 1872.

From an account of the "Women's National Suffrage Association," reported to the Press, I cut the following description of a noted female doctress who dresses in a garb as near to a man's as the cramped laws of the land will admit.

"Ten minutes after the opening . . . a curly, crinkly feminine, in very large walking boots, came to the front, being followed, after a brief pause, by the rest of the sisters. This lady was new, even to the reporters, and one of them, handing up a pencilled inquiry to Mrs. Dr. Walker, was informed that she was ' Mrs. Ricker, a beautiful, charming, and good widow, fair, forty, and rich." This bit of interesting news started on its travels.

.   .   .   .   .

"The doctor, who has the usual manly proclivity for hugging the girls, threw her arms around a pretty and modest-looking girl standing by, and enthusiastically shouted, "You are a dear, sweet little creature." The frightened young woman drew hastily back, and faltered out that she was not in the habit of being hugged by men. This turned the laugh on the doctor; but she gained her lost ground by quickly replying to the inquiry of the secretary as to what place he should put her down from as a delegate, to put her down "from all the world;" but he objected, anxious for the completeness of his roster.

Figure 7.1 The Funny Side of Physic (1874).

Other book sources

There are many online sources that offer books for free, purchase or rental. Most draw on content published by the three sites detailed above as well as their own sources. The benefit of using multiple sites is that one search engine may pick up references missed by others. Varying results offer the researcher a great choice of material. Use search terms consistently across different resources. As most search engines feature the most relevant returns at the top of the search results, it is possible to limit the screening process to a set number of pages, e.g., the first 100 results.

A few other book sources include:

- *Europeana* links to roughly 10 million digital objects from over 1,000 archives in the European Union. The site has clever short-cuts to aid in searches.

  - *who:* – Type the word 'who' followed by a colon before a name to find materials created or written by a particular individual. For example, 'who: Edward Carpenter'.
  - *what:* – Type the word 'what' followed by a colon and a search term to retrieve non-textual material, such as maps or topics.
  - *where:* – 'Where' followed by a colon and a search term will return items relating to a location.
  - *when:* – 'When' followed by a colon and a date will return items which have a date in the title or description.

- *Gallica* is an extensive French digital library which includes books, newspapers, manuscripts, maps, images and other digitised materials. While a publication identified through a search does not automatically open at the pertinent page, if you input a keyword(s) search, the relevant page number will be given. Much of the content is, of course, in French. To translate texts into English, try using the *Snipping Tool*, converting the material to text via a free OCR reader app and then running the text through an online translator.

- *National Digital Library of India* (NDLI) integrates several national and international digital libraries in English and Indian languages. It is free to register and download public-domain material. It does not have a particularly good search engine. Neither quotation marks nor Boolean commands work, but it does link to other digital libraries in Asia.

- *Runivers* is a Russian digital library. Due to the state's attitude towards LGBTQIA+ there are not many returns. Search results are usually taken from other sources.

- *Wikisource* is on online library of free material from sources which Google Books, Project Gutenberg and Internet Archive tend not to use. A lot of Asian material can be recovered. Similarly, *Wikicommons* is a source of public-domain images.

- *World Digital Library* is operated by UNESCO and the United States Library of Congress. It aims to expand free access to international cultural content. The returns are beautifully presented with a textual background to the book and the relevant page illustrated, which saves on opening multiple pages. While some returns are interesting, LGBTQIA+ searches currently provide limited results.

Additional websites with digitalised collections include: *Biblio Vault: A Scholarly Book Repository, Digital.Bodlean, Digital Public Library of America* (DPLA), *epubBooks, Google News, Harvard Digital Collections, HathiTrust, Internet Public Library* (IPL), *Library of Congress, Morgan Library and Museum, Munich DigitiZation Centre* (MDZ), *Smithsonian Learning Lab, United Nations Digital Library, Universal Digital Library* and *Wellcome Library.*

Cataloguing books

There are a number of tools and sites which allow members, either as individuals or organisations, to create and upload catalogues of books, CDs, films and other works. Examples include *BookAuthority, Bookicious, Bookshelf – Your Virtual Library, Goodreads, inventaire.io, Leafmarks, lib. reviews, Library Thing, MyAnimeList* and many more. Creating a 'My Library' list allows the user to collate existing titles and share the list, which may aid research on specific topics and other researchers.

For those who want to catalogue hard-copy collections, there are apps for phones and tablets that scan a book's barcode and automatically generate a citation, which can be saved in a Word document, spreadsheet or elsewhere. For books with no bar codes or damaged editions, the details need to be typed in by hand. Some devices may struggle with bar codes, as the tools rely on cameras rather than scanners. They never work as efficiently as the scanners seen in shops. A large array of bar code scanning apps are available. A number of the cataloguing sites provide basic versions for free, while more advanced versions come at a cost. Alternatively, search for '*book cataloguing software*' or '*bar code scanning apps*' on the internet. Some apps also compare scanned titles to content on shopping platforms, allowing users to make price comparisons. In this way personal collections can then be uploaded to book sites, and lists can be shared between users.

Copyright

It is essential to remember that while a book is free to download, it may not be copyright free. Always check before reusing an image or extensive extracts of text. Even if a book in the public domain is free, whoever scanned it and put it online owns the copyright to the image. The image cannot be reproduced without the copyright holder's permission even though the text itself can be freely used.

Just because a publication is old and out of copyright does not mean it is available to be viewed. Unless someone has selected it, scanned it and uploaded it, it will not be available. Many books still in copyright, particularly those of the late twentieth century, are difficult to find in libraries, digital collections and sales sites.

It is often believed that 'fair use' allows writers to quote up to a certain number of words from a publication, however quotation amounts are often controlled by the publisher. While many have no objections to a small number of words being quoted, larger selections often need the permission of the publisher. In the UK and other countries, copyright is in effect for the author's lifetime plus 70 years. If a work is by multiple authors, the 70 years does not start until the death of the last author. As of 1 January 2020, most material published or released in the United States prior to 1924 is automatically in the public domain, and annually the date increases by a year.

The creation of collections can generate a new copyright. While each work itself may be in the public domain, if they are put together to form a new work, the new work's copyright belongs to the collection's editors or creators. For example, a book of LGBTQIA+ poems may include individual free-to-use poems, but copying and distributing the complete collection may infringe 'collective works' copyright.

If photographing a page from a publication owned by an organisation, such as a library, archive or museum, be aware that permission may be required from the owners of the item. Cultural institutions have different rules regarding photography for research purposes as well as the use of images for publication. Always check with the organisation to determine permission requirements.

Journals, papers and dissertations

Academic journal articles can be notoriously difficult for the average researcher to access. Universities hold extensive collections that are available to researchers with readers' tickets. University collections reflect the institutions' specialisms and are usually located in major towns or cities.

Most academic journals are digitally published. Access is often restricted to collections that are limited to institutional subscribers, such as EBSCO Academic Search Premier, Gale Academic One File,

Gale Archives Unbound; JSTOR, Project MUSE, SAGE Journals, Scholar One Search, Taylor & Francis Online and many others too numerous to list here. Online sites and journal collections differ in specialisms, such as medicine, science or culture, which can assist in targeting results. For researchers affiliated with an educational facility or public library, digital access may be free as long as the institution subscribes to a provider. If the institution is not a subscriber, the site may allow fee-based access to read articles, although the charges can be extremely high. It may be useful to search sites and journal collections, despite being denied access, because you can identify papers and determine if they are accessible elsewhere for free. The more searches undertaken, the more material recovered.

Some sites do include free, open-access material, such as Access to Research, Google Scholar, Microsoft Academic, National Center for Biotechnology Information (NCBI), 'open content' on JSTOR, SAGE Open, WorldWideScience.org and many more. To find similar sites search for 'academic papers free content', 'free online journals and research', 'open access journals' or similar. Sites offering papers on a myriad of subjects include Core, Directory of Open Access Journals, Dryad, Jurn, OpenDoar and many others.

It is worth checking individual countries to see what archives they offer. The ArQuives, for example, is 'Canada's LGBTQ2+ Archives'.

Some sites provide registered members tools to assist with research, such as the ability to save searches or set up preferences. If signing up for free membership, check what notification services the site provides. Some will send notices of new papers according to the researcher's logged preference, while others automatically send papers of interest.

While most general journal sites do not have a dedicated LGBTQIA+ sections, some do. ProQuest, for example, has an 'LGBT Magazine Archive' with runs of 26 of the most influential, long-running, twentieth- and twenty-first-century magazines published in the United States. However, access is only possible via an organisation or institution that subscribes to the database.

A general internet search for 'LGBTQIA+ academic journals' or similar will provide a list of either dedicated titles, such as the *Journal of Homosexuality, Journal of Bisexuality* or *Journal of Lesbian Studies*, or journals that regularly include papers on sexual orientation and gender diversity.

To stay up-to-date on recent research trends and subjects, search the internet 'LGBTQIA+ conferences', 'LGBTQIA+ call for papers', 'submissions' or similar. This is particularly effective in the build up to and during LGBT+ History Month, the annual celebration of all historical aspects of sexual orientation and gender diversity. Currently, a month-long observance is celebrated in the UK (February), USA (October) and Canada (October), while other countries hold events over a shorter period or combine it with annual Pride celebrations. Also, in most internet search engines a drop-down list of popular searches will appear as keyword(s) are being typed, which can illustrate what topics are trending.

Magazines

Wikipedia has a list of international 'LGBT periodicals', both current and out of print. It also offers a page of 'British LGBT-related magazines' and similar country-specific lists. Some of the well-known titles associated with the 'Pink Press' are named, but it is a short list and does not include lesser-known or regional publications, such as *Gay Scotland*.

Modern magazines

Almost all popular international magazines available today have searchable content, particularly from the 2000s onwards. Some results are available to read online. For most a subscription is needed, which is available either directly from the magazine website or through organisations which bundle titles for a single subscription price. A basic internet search for 'magazine subscriptions' will result in myriad returns for sites which offer such services.

Some libraries provide access to subscription sites, such as Press-Reader or RBdigital Magazines, which offer a large selection of newspapers, magazines, audio books and comics in various languages for users to access remotely or on the premises. Users with a library membership number can login via the participating library or the provider itself, although some libraries only permit access on the premises through their public computers. Not all libraries use the same providers, so membership in several libraries will likely give greater access. Check each library's website to see what resources are offered.

It can be useful to regularly check the e-resources offered on a library website. The status of resources may change. For example, *European Sources Online* (ESO) is a very useful site which aims to support research and understanding on any matter relating to Europe. Keyword(s) searches will suggest topics and provide a background summaries of issues. Results can be filtered via country, content type, subject or organisation. Originally a subscription service, it is now free to all, although some libraries still show it as only being available on their premises.

Back issues

Digitalising back issues is a costly and lengthy process, which means many publications from the mid- to late-twentieth century are not available. Because little is accessible online, researchers must often visit a holding library, purchase back copies or pay to join one of the many magazine subscription sites. If it is necessary to subscribe, try doing so at periods when special offers are available, such Black Friday or Christmas.

Magazines from the second half of the twentieth century can provide interesting research possibilities. Many contained 'agony columns', which include letters from readers seeking advice on sexual orientation or gender identity. Content can be examined to look at the way LGBTQIA+ people were represented or sensationalised during this period. Personal ads are another research area that has not been extensively covered to date.

Few institutions carry complete runs of the leading UK LGBTQIA+ magazines published between 1970 and 2000. To find a local or nearby collection, enter a postcode into *WorldCat* and conduct a search. Some early archives are being digitalised. The *Gay News Archive Project*, a volunteer-based initiative, currently contains only the years 1972/3. It does allow copies to be downloaded. These early issues are useful for studying local venues and personal ads. Some publications are available on Internet Archive, such as copies of *Gay Times* and *Diva*, mainly from the 2000s, as well as American publications, such as *Gay Community News* from the 1970s.

Grey literature

Originally, the term 'grey literature' referred to reports, conference proceedings and doctoral theses. It has expanded, however, to include unpublished material and non-commercial publications where publishing is not the prime activity of the producing body. This can include government reports, white papers, conference papers, newsletters, evaluations, technical reports, unpublished manuscripts, patents, personal communications, lecture notes and so on. The term covers an extensive list of document types.

The importance of grey literature is that it includes many niche areas which may not be covered by commercial publishers. It can also be more current than commercial publications, which have lengthy pro-duction cycles. Some need months for preparation or peer-review prior to publication. While much grey literature is of a high standard, it can have downsides, such as a lack of oversight, control, accuracy, peer-review, citations, bibliographical information or copyright notices. Caution and more thorough evaluation are advised. An internet search for 'grey literature sources' will result in a number of sites offering material and internal search engines. Some sites can be short lived. It is therefore advisable to download or copy content in case either it or the site disappears.

Getting LGBTQIA+ material published in general commercial publications is often quite difficult. As such, research will often appear in grey literature.

IHLIA Open Up! has collected and digitized about 95,000 pages of LGBTQIA+ documents. Its online content may be viewed via a free membership. If online content is considered sensitive, an application needs to be submitted explaining why access is required. Some content can only be viewed at the organisation's premises in Amsterdam.

Other electronic publishing platforms exist. *Issuu*, for example, allows for the basic, entry-level uploading of digital publications. Its magazines and other content are usually free to read. They are mainly arranged in categories, few of which include LGBTQIA+ subjects. Search options are not always available. Searching for 'online maga-zines' will produce a list of the myriad companies selling subscriptions to current publications. Some databases dedicated to LGBTQIA+ research, such as *LGBT Life with Full Text, LGBT Studies in Video* and *LGBT Thought and Culture*, are only accessible via an academic login.

The websites of most public bodies, organisations and institutions will include some grey literature. The range of publications is vast. Their content and quality can vary enormously.

A small sample of council websites illustrates differences in the quality of grey literature for LGBTQIA+ people. For example, a search for 'LGBT' on the Essex Council publications website produces 58 returns, none of which are content specific. Instead, pages on var-ious subjects are included. Clicking on a sample selection reveals that the content has no information on LGBTQIA+ subjects, making it difficult to understand the returns. The Council's plans and strategies include nothing on LGBTQIA+. An identical search on the Powys Council website results in one link to 'our social media sites', which simply leads to other sites with no guarantee of any content. The same search on the Aberdeenshire Council website produces no results.

In contrast, the 'LGBT' keyword search on the Derbyshire County Council website results in 15 returns. The Council publishes its intentions to fly the rainbow flag during celebratory days and months:

Flying the rainbow is one way to show that we don't tolerate homophobia or transphobia. We want our workplaces, schools and communities to be safe places where everyone is able to be themselves without fear of bullying, intimidation, abuse or harm.

('Equalities and Diversity Events' 2020)

The Leicestershire Council website returns 12 relevant hits, while the Edinburgh Council site generates 116 hits of dedicated and non-dedicated content. A page on the Edinburgh Council site includes a management review of *Easter Craiglockhart Hill Local Nature Reserve* that lists LGBT people as a target audience.

Many organisations produce a Strategic Equality Plan (SEP) or Strategic Plan. Not all organisations refer to such plans as SEPs. Some are called Equality and Diversity Policies/Plans or similar. Most are reviewed every one to five years. Finding content can be difficult, however, and not all documents reference LGBTQIA+ issues. The Northamptonshire Council SEP estimates the LGBTQIA+ population of their county. In contrast, North Yorkshire and Powys have no LGBTQIA+ content in their SEPs, showing how variable such content can be. All of these results are as of the time of writing, but it would be interesting to analyse materials produced by British councils to identify those that make an effort to provide content for and address the needs of local LGBTQIA+ people.

Other useful public sources include transcripts of political and legislative debates as well as statutes. Legislative publications from the UK include *Hansard* for the proceedings of the UK Parliament, the electronic *Irish Statute Book* (eISB) for the Tithe an Oireachtas (Ireland's national parliament), the *Journal of the Scottish Parliament*, the *Official Report (Hansard)* for the Northern Ireland Assembly and the *Record of Proceedings* for The National Assembly for Wales. All these records are free to access online and are valuable sources for tracking LGBTQIA+ political debates. Debates on Wolfenden (1957) and same-sex marriage (2014) can be read in full. Searches for individual MPs can identify their comments and opinions. *Hansard* includes material relating to some commonwealth countries. Most democratic nations publish their political debates, although not all will be accessible online.

Student newsletters, newspapers published by universities and materials produced by university LGBTQIA+ societies often include relevant content. Some universities have digitalised current and archival material. For example, Bangor created a digital archive for *Y Seren* (*The Star*), its monthly student newspaper, which includes a large amount of LBGTQIA+ content and is particularly useful for studies of the 1980s. *The Oxford Student* has a dedicated 'Pink' tab for their current and recent issues, but there are no archived copies from its inception in 1991. The website for Cambridge University's *Varsity*, which was founded in 1947, includes a large amount of relevant content but no archival copies are available. A search for 'LGBT' on the site for Cardiff University's paper, *Gair Rhydd* (*Free Word*), also produces a large number of returns. In 2012 the paper started archiving back copies on *Issuu*, and the collection includes 'stacks' of the newspaper published between 2000 and 2020 as well as copies of *Quench*, the University's monthly lifestyle magazine (Cardiff Student Media 2020).

Conclusion

Finding hard copies of LGBTQIA+ material can be difficult. Collections are limited, and researchers often have to travel to access libraries or other cultural institutions. However, a vast amount of material is available to be discovered via various platforms on the internet.

Even with online materials there are difficulties, such as the suppression of disinterest. In order for a work to be included in Google Books, Internet Archive and other sites, someone must decide to scan and upload it. It is time consuming and expensive to scan a work to a professional standard. Materials related to LGBTQIA+ studies are not digitised and do not appear with the same frequency as other areas of study. Materials in languages other than English are neglected. For example, works by French writers from the end of the nineteenth century, particularly those writing during the Decadent Movement, receive little attention in digitalised collections. Marc de Montifaud (Marie-Amélie Chartroule de Montifaud, 1845–1912) and 'Rachilde' (Marguerite Vallette-Eymery, 1860–1953) wrote works which challenged sexuality and gender. However, obtaining copies of their works is very difficult. Rachilde's *Monsieur Venus* (1884) is a highly erotic and scandalous work. The theme of gender subversion dominates the story. It is a book which influenced other writers. Oscar Wilde, for example, named the book that Dorian Gray reads *Le Secret de Raoul*, which is taken from Rachilde's main character, Raoule de Vénérande. French and English versions are available on online book sites and bookstores, but they are not tagged as being of gender fluidity interest.

Accuracy is a persistent problem. Simply because a publication exists does not guarantee that the material can be relied upon. Publications can date very quickly as new information emerges or research improves. Authors can get things wrong. Authors have agendas, such as the far-right groups that publish misinformation and hatred about LGBTQIA+ people. Copyright issues and individuals uploading material on publication platforms can also pose difficulties. Some people plagiarise material and present it as their own, so checking may be necessary.

Despite these difficulties, there is still a lot to discover. If help is required, it may be useful to join the LGBTQ+ Network of the Chartered Institute of Library and Information Professionals (CILIP), which was established to 'provide guidance, support and a safe space to share knowledge and experiences for library, information and knowledge workers who identify as LGBTQ+' (CILIP LGBTQ+ Network 2020).

Bibliography

Cardiff Student Media (CSM). (2020). *ISSUU: Cardiff Student Media (CSM)*. Accessed online at https://issuu.com/gairrhydd/stacks

CILIP LGBTQ+ Network. (2020). 'LGBTQ+ Network.' *CILIP: The Library and Information Association*. Accessed online at https://www.cilip.org.uk/members/group_content_view.asp?group=226845&id=864499&hhSearchTerms=%22lgbtq%22

Crabtree, Addison Darre. (1874). *The Funny Side of Physic: Or, The Mysteries of Medicine*. Hartford, CT: The J. B. Burr Publishing Co. p. 713.

Flood, Alison. (2019). 'Stonewall Defends 'Vital' LGBT Children's Books after Spate of Ban Attempts.' *The Guardian*. 18 January.

'Equalities and Diversity Events.' (2020). *Derbyshire County Council*. Accessed online at https://www.derbyshire.gov.uk/council/equalities/sexual-orientation/idaho/equalities-and-diversity-events.aspx

Gregg, J. & Rindinger, R.B.M. (Eds.). (1988). *International Thesaurus of Gay and Lesbian Index Terms*. Chicago: Thesaurus Committee, Gay and Lesbian Task Force, American Library Association.

Johnson, Matt. (2007). 'GLBT Controlled Vocabularies and Classification Schemes.' *American Library Association: Rainbow Round Table (RRT)*. Accessed online at http://www.ala.org/rt/rrt/popularresources/vocab

'LTBT+ Library Resources: Other Libraries and Archives.' (2020). *University of Reading: Library/LibGuides*. Accessed online at https://libguides.reading.ac.uk/LGBT/other_libraries

Shopland, Norena & Leeworthy, Daryl. (2018). *Queering Glamorgan: A Research Guide to Sources for the Study of LGBT History.* Glamorgan Archives. Accessed online at https://glamarchives.gov.uk/wp-content/uploads/2018/08/Queering-Glamorgan-28Aug2018.pdf

Vincent, John. (2013). *LGBT People and the UK Cultural Sector: The Response of Libraries, Museums, Archives and Heritage Since 1950.* Farnham: Ashgate Publishing Limited. doi:10.4324/9781315592282.

8 Researching in archives

Wikipedia has a 'List of Archives' covering numerous countries, but few of the links work. The International Council on Archives (ICA) has 1,400 institutional members in 199 countries and territories. Searches for various keyword(s) on the ICA website will return interesting material. For example, a search for 'homosexual' results in links to many newsletters published by the ICA or its Human Rights Working Group (HRWG), which provide short updates on what is happening in their member archives and pertinent information from the general news. The newsletter of March 2013, for example, reports that the complete archive covering the treason trial of Captain Alfred Dreyfus in France was digitalized and uploaded to the Internet, including information about 'homosexual liaisons between certain actors in the affair' (Peterson 2013). It is worth checking international archives, but access both online and in person may vary.

The last few decades have seen an increase in the number of dedicated LGBTQIA+ archives, many of which include global material, so it is worth consulting as many as possible.

This chapter considers British archives, but the methods outlined can be used in most organizations of a similar nature.

Archives

There are three national repositories in the UK: The National Archives, National Records of Scotland and the Public Records Office of Northern Ireland (PRONI). For Ireland there is An Cartlann Náisiúnta – National Archives of Ireland. Wales does not have a national archive.

In addition, there are hundreds of local archives along with those held in universities, other educational facilities, businesses, charities, local authorities, museums, police forces, societies and specialist collections at health facilities, arts centres and elsewhere.

The content of archives also varies considerably and can include printed and handwritten material, digitally produced content, photographs, audiovisual material, maps, material objects and much more.

With such a bewildering array, where does one start?

Many archives are publicly accessible. For those who have never visited or used one, there are helpful staff on hand to aid researchers.

Most archives provide clear instructions on how to use their facilities and explain archival terminology. Other advice can be obtained from online sites and articles, such as the 'Resources About Archives' (2020) page on the JISC *Archives Hub* website, 'Using Archives: A Guide to Effective Research' by Laura Schmidt (2016), 'Queering the Archive: Transforming the Archival Process' by Lizeth Zepeda (2018), the 'Archival Research' *Wikipedia* entry and many others.

A number of matters need to be considered and compiled with before visiting an archive, such as reader registration procedures and identification requirements. Always check the relevant organisation's guidelines before visiting.

Access to modern records may be restricted under the Data Protection Act, meaning that many items and files are closed for 75 years from the date of deposit. Materials less than 100 years old may be restricted. Limitations vary, and it may be possible to obtain permission to consult records depending on the purpose of your research, so always discuss access and permissions with staff members.

There are a few general websites which may help identify archives holding information according to keyword(s) searches:

- *AIM25* is an educational charity that provides a portal for searching over 100 institutional repositories within London and the M25 area. No historic LGBTQIA+ keyword(s) produce search results. However, there are returns for modern terms, which are mainly linked to the London School of Economics (LSE) and the London Metropolitan Archives (LMA).
- *Discovery* (previously *Access to Archives* (A2A)) is the search tool of The National Archives. In addition to cataloguing National Archives materials, it includes records from more than 2,500 archives throughout England and Wales. Some materials are available for direct download. Searches in *Discovery* return hits linked to partner archives, but LGBTQIA+ returns are few and predominantly modern.
- *Archives Hub*, which accesses the catalogues of 350 organisations across the UK, returns few or no hits for female keywords. A search for 'homosexuality' returns 162 collections in 27

repositories: 19 in South East England, two in Scotland and six in the Midlands. Manchester has 42 collections, followed by 34 at the LSE, 25 at Newcastle and 12 at the Glasgow's Women's Library. The remaining 49 are spread between 23 repositories, with eight listing only one item.

General archives

One of the barriers to accessing archival collections is location. Most county archives are situated in a main town or city, but travelling to these may be difficult or cost prohibitive for certain individuals. Some archives do provide research services, but they generally involve fees. Archives have varying policies regarding registration, photography, copying, laptops and items that can be brought into the reading room, so always consult websites before visiting.

When visiting archives, either online or in person, it is worth bearing in mind that catalogues tend to include brief, overview descriptions of record types, not complete transcripts or reproductions of individual documents. Therefore, listings may not contain standard keyword(s). Often only the collection name is recorded, such as an individual or organisation. Online catalogues are continually being updated, so it is worth checking regularly. It is hoped that in the future archive catalogues will provide opportunities for including more LGBTQIA+ tagging. Generally speaking, most archival research needs to be done in person at the relevant repository.

Accessing a collection or document does not mean it can be reproduced. There may be limitations with regard to copyright or data protection issues related to identifiable individuals.

National archives

The National Archives (TNA) is the official UK repository of governmental records and significant publications or documents of national interest. TNA includes records created by the government regarding LGBTQIA+ matters as well as other significant material. The TNA website includes a 'How to Look for Records of Sexuality and Gender Identity History' (2020) research guide with suggested historical terms and links to podcasts as well as a dedicated 'LGBT History' page.

For searches TNA uses *Discovery*, a UK-wide database that links users to TNA materials and the catalogues of 2,500 other repositories – more than those listed on Wikipedia. The results of keyword(s) searches in *Discovery* mostly relate to men. Keyword(s) related to women seem to be restricted to 'lesbian'. Terms such as 'tribade', 'sapphist' and 'sapphism' returned no hits. Similarly, there are no returns for 'bisexual' or for a variety of trans keywords. A search for 'hermaphrodite' produces only six hits.

The National Library of Wales is predominantly a library, but it does contain the largest collection of Welsh archival materials, including over 4,000 manuscripts and the National Screen and Sound Archive of Wales. It describes itself as 'The Nation's Memory – collecting, preserving and giving access to Welsh history and culture'. Researching LGBTQIA+ history is primarily restricted to library listings and predominantly modern publications.

The National Records of Scotland, despite having a rather clunky website, offers interesting search returns. Some results are drawn directly from archival records. For example, a search for 'sodomy' produces 64 results from nineteenth- and twentieth-century criminal records, while 'homosexual' returns 216 twentieth-century results. Again, women are poorly served. 'Lesbian' is the only keyword that produces results, with seven records. A search for 'bisexual' has one result. There are no returns for a variety of trans keyword(s), including 'hermaphrodite'.

A search for 'sodomy' in the eCatalogue of PRONI, the Public Record Office of Northern Ireland, generates only two returns from the eighteenth and twentieth centuries. 'Homosexual' generates 34 results, while 'lesbian' returns only two, both related to a closed file on a befriending group for lesbian, gay and bisexual people. The befriending group appears again in searches for 'bisexual' and 'transvestite', but no other trans-related keyword(s), including 'hermaphrodite', produce results. For gay women, bisexuals and trans people, there is only one item in the PRONI public records.

For An Cartlann Náisiúnta – National Archives of Ireland, the only keyword(s) search that provided any results was 'sexual orientation', which identified two papers on discrimination in employment from 2014 and 2016.

Similar results can be found elsewhere. Catalogue search results in Archives New Zealand, Library and Archives Canada and the New York State Archives rarely exceeded 20 returns. The National Archives of Australia returns mixed results. There was nothing for 'bisexual', four results for 'transgender', 110 for 'lesbian' and 1,988 for 'gay', although a number of these results included personal names and definitions not related to sexual orientation.

Obviously, these results are from online catalogues only, and much more material will exist in the archives.

Local archives

There are over 700 national and local archives in the UK. Many are listed on the 'List of Archives in the United Kingdom' *Wikipedia* page, which provides links to the organisations. Searches in a sample selection of local archives produces results similar to those obtained in national archives. No – or few – keyword(s) returns are found. For example, inputting modern and some older terms into the online catalogues of the Dorset History Centre and the Derbyshire Record Office returns no hits at all. The Kressen Kernow ('Cornwall Centre') archive catalogue produced one result for 'gay' from 2002, two results for 'sodomy', nothing for other modern keywords and little else. *The South West Heritage Trust: Somerset Archive Catalogue* is upfront about its lack of information. Its 'Lesbian, Gay, Bisexual and Trans (LGBT) History' (2020) research guide states, 'Little specific research has been done on LGBT history in Somerset', and the lack of returns on the search page supports this.

Some archives do provide fair to excellent support for local LGBTQIA+ researchers wishing to explore their history, but they are in the minority. Glamorgan Archives provides the *Queering Glamorgan* (2018) LGBTQIA+ research guide, actively collects materials and reaches out to local groups and individuals. Lancashire Archives offers a research guide, 'Handlist 73 – Sources for LGBT History' (2011), and its catalogue returns many hits for keyword(s) searches. Surrey County Council Archives and Libraries have excellent and extensive coverage of LGBTQIA+ sources, including lists of local LGBTQIA+ people with biographies, an 'Out Lit – Our LGBT Collections' (2020) reading list and links to local and national support organisations and groups. They also have a page dedicated to the history of GAGS (Guildford Area Gay Society) one of the country's earliest gay groups founded in 1977.

What can be found in archives

There are a vast number of possible collections within archives to search through. Not all can be covered here. The following provides some suggestions of the sorts of records to look for, and what can be found within them.

Crime

LGBTQIA+ history has been and continues to be dominated by the male narrative. This is true of women's history generally. For example, women represent just under 18 percent of the total number of individual biographies on *Wikipedia*.

The male narrative, in turn, tends to be dominated by criminal records, as homosexuality was against the law for much of history. Only after 1967 did men find some freedom to be who they were. However, even after decriminalisation it continued to be socially unacceptable to be LGBTQIA+, so much of the record is hidden even after the late 1960s.

Crime records are divided into numerous collections. Perhaps the most well-known ones relate to arrests, court appearances and imprisonment.

Prior to the Buggery Act of 1852–54, same-sex offences were dealt with by the church in its ecclesiastical courts, usually under the offence of sodomy. In reality, few same-sex offences were included in prosecutions for sodomy.

As industrialisation grew and people migrated to areas with more employment opportunities, crime (and criminal records) increased. Search results tend to be found in urban areas rather than rural ones. Modern policing began in the 1830s, and the prosecution of crime subsequently shifted from private individuals to the state.

Criminal records can consist of calendars of prisoners, session rolls, prison and felony registers, indictment rolls as well as records from quarter sessions and magistrates' courts. Details included in the records can vary enormously. They may include names, descriptions of the summons, witness statements, bail records, information about where a crime took place or details about who was involved and where they lived. A complete record from arrest to imprisonment rarely survives.

Many of those accused of male same-sex activity were acquitted through lack of evidence. Sodomy could only be an offence if ejaculation and/or penetration took place, which required witnesses to the act. However, when witnesses were asked to convict someone known locally to either many years in prison or death (until 1861), they were often reluctant to give evidence. In cases lacking evidence, the charge could be reduced to the lesser offence of 'assault with sodomitical intent' – a charge often shortened to 'assault' in public texts or reading material.

Care needs to be taken when considering cases of sodomy, unnatural crimes, gross indecency or other similar acts because the terms covered a broad range of crimes. When a single name is mentioned, for example, more research is needed to prove that a case refers to a same-sex couple.

Crimes involving women and trans individuals are more extensively recovered when keyword(s) and phrases related to cross-dressing and cross-living are used.

Modern, twentieth-century records tend to be more extensive than those from any other period. Searches have greater returns, and information on arrests, 'cottaging' or assignations involving men in public toilets, venues, pubs, clubs or public spaces can indicate where men were meeting. Many of these records will be closed under the Data Protection Act, but some information may be accessible after discussions with archivists.

Most criminal records are not available online. Those which have been digitalised are not extensive, meaning research must be undertaken within physical archives. The following examples of types of criminal records are arranged alphabetically rather than in the order that events typically took place in a criminal case.

Assizes

More serious cases were referred to the assize courts, which were held twice a year and overseen by professional judges. Counties were grouped into circuits, which consisted of the Home, Norfolk and South-Eastern Circuits; Midland Circuit; Northern and North-Eastern Circuits; Oxford Circuit; Welsh Circuits, including Chester and Western Circuit. The equivalent to the assizes in Wales is referred to as the Court of Great Sessions, the records of which are held in the National Library Wales. It operated between 1542 to 1830, when it was replaced by assizes.

At the 9 March 1857 York Assizes, Christopher Good, a 26-year-old labourer, was convicted of sodomy. He was sentenced to death, but the sentence was commuted to life. On 21 June 1861, a licence was granted for his early release from Millbank Prison.[1] In 1910 at the Kent Assizes, Frederick Fidler and Charles Bird were tried for attempted sodomy. The Assizes file includes a brief for the prosecution and depositions of witnesses.[2]

Cases should always be checked, even when two male names appear, as wives could be represented by their husbands in court.

The assizes were abolished in 1956 and replaced by Crown Courts. Many of the English assize court records are held at The National Archives.

Other information can be found in bills of costs, the fees paid to solicitors. For example, a bill of costs exists for the 1875 prosecution of Francis Moran and William Pye for attempting to commit buggery.[3]

Some information also may be found in the files of legal representatives. Records in the Carlisle Archives for Waugh and Musgrave, solicitors of Cockermouth, include papers from a 1945 case in

Whitehaven: Crown v. John Sharp of Salterbeck, in which a single, 44-year-old locomotive fireman was accused of gross indecency with Stanley Harry, a 33-year-old sailor in the Merchant Navy.[4]

Calendars of prisoners

Calendars of prisoners are, for the most part, annual lists of prisoners tried at assizes and quarter sessions that can include useful details, such as names, ages, occupations, where offences took place and some information about previous convictions. Not all records are detailed. Some contain only the basics, such as the 1812 Lancashire Archives calendar of prisoners listing for Hartley Blackburn, 26, who was accused of the 'unnatural crime of sodomy'. There was no prosecution, but checks would need to be made as to what kind of sodomy Blackburn was accused of committing.[5]

Other offences may be described as 'unnatural'. For example, in 1834 John Taylor, 56, was found guilty of committing 'an unnatural crime with a certain other man at present unknown.'[6]

Indictment Rolls

Details of the formal charges made against an individual may be found in the indictment rolls. These can sometimes contain more information about the individual than other criminal records. For example, in 1753 a charge against William Lomax, an innkeeper of Blackrod, alleged that he

> by force and arms at Blackrod in and upon Bernard Gornall … did strike beat wound and much abuse so that of his life it was despaired with an intent that most detestable horrid and sodomitical crime called buggery with and to the great damage of the said Bernard Gornall against the Orders of Nature.[7]

Petty sessions

Running from the 1730s to 1872, petty sessions were local magistrates courts that dealt with minor matters and decided whether a case should be escalated to a quarter session.

Police records

Local police records are held in relevant archives, and their scope and content can be obtained from the archive.

When viewing archival materials concerning the arrest of men, be alert for a doctor's name. They were often brought in for physical examinations, and their names may appear among witnesses in court cases.. If there is uncertainty as to what type of sodomy a case concerns, a reference to a physician may indicate homosexuality, as doctors often examined a man's anus for loose or smooth skin, a widening of the aperture and other features. The theory regarding evidence of homosexual activity was developed by Auguste Ambroise Tardieu in 1857. It was deeply flawed but remained in use for many years after being completely discredited. There is no consistent evidence that can prove anal sex, and a 'loose' anus can have a variety of causes. However, such examinations are still being used in a variety of countries, despite the UN Committee Against Torture saying that they have no medical justification and campaigners insisting that they violate international law (Burke 2018).

Quarter sessions

Between 1833 and 1972 (1975 in Scotland), courts of quarter sessions sat four times a year, as indicated by the name, in county and borough seats. Information about their activities are found in quarter session records and quarter session rolls (originally rolls of paper). The courts considered both minor criminal and civil cases and usually were overseen by magistrates. Civil cases, which could be brought by any member of the public, were usually recorded in the court's order books, while criminal cases were recorded in indictment books. A range of quarter sessions records are found in archives, including session rolls, presentments, recognizances, depositions of witnesses, examinations of the accused and others.

Cases are recorded chronologically, which makes it easy to cross-check reports published elsewhere, such as in the newspapers.

Some online archive catalogues refer only to 'sessions'. For example, a search in TNA's *Discovery* returned a 'Lancashire Sessions' record for John Dennett, who was prosecuted on two charges of buggery for which he received ten years and then life in prison.[8] Other catalogue entries specifically reference 'quarter sessions'. Some archival references begin with or include the initials 'QS'. The Kresen Kernow ('Cornwall Centre') catalogue reference number for the 1893 Bodmin quarter sessions record for Thomas Sweet, who confessed to attempted sodomy on William Hedley Holman on 17 December 1892 and received hard labour for six months, is QS/1/21/212.[9]

It is worth bearing in mind that LGBTQIA+ material may be found by considering not who the individual was but what they were doing.

For example, in the eighteenth century Mary Hamilton became well-known as a 'female husband' after supposedly marrying several women. She can be traced in Somerset's quarter sessions. Hamilton had married Mary Price at Wells in 1746. On discovering her new husband was a woman, Price sued, and the case went to trial.[10]

Blackmail cases may also be found. Section 11 of the Criminal Law Amendment Act (1885) was known as 'the blackmailer's charter' due to the ease with which people could be accused. However, much earlier cases can be found in quarter sessions records. For example, in 1821 Susan Swift from Buckingham was prosecuted for sending threatening letters to Mainwaring Davies 'with the purpose of extorting money from him, charging him with the crime of sodomy.' She was found not guilty.[11]

Local authority records

Official papers of various councils, parish vestries and boards of local authorities may be available. In accordance with the data protection laws, some may be open to view. Content could include debates around services, facilities, protection and support at a local level. Records may reflect the prevailing views of the times. These could be cross-referenced with police records, information from venues or meeting places and newspaper reports.

Parish and religious records

Early parish registers information can be limited. They are mostly handwritten and may include Latin terms. From 1813 records were standardised with pre-printed pages.

Before 1837, when civil registration was introduced, parish registers of religious bodies represent a comprehensive, chronological source of information. The records and their locations are very varied. They include not just births, deaths and marriages (BDMs) but also baptisms, burials and Bishop's transcripts. The Somerset Parish Records record the 1732 burial of Frances, a hermaphrodite child of Thomas and Mary Hillier.[12] The same records also contain an entry for the 14 January 1817 marriage of Henry Stoake, described as a bachelor, and Ann Hants at the Sheffield Parish Church. However, the original name filled in by the groom was Harriet, which was crossed out and replaced with Henry, possibly indicating a same-sex marriage.

Some archives have collected modern material from civil partnerships and same-sex marriages. Details of Mark and Sigurd's 2007 wedding/blessing celebrations, for example, can be found in Glouces-tershire Archives.[13] Consultations around same-sex marriage, often referred to as 'equal marriage', were undertaken by the British Gov-ernment, but they were predominantly in England. Only one consulta-tion was held in Wales, and a detailed report on the event is held at Glamorgan Archives.[14]

For fleshing out information about individuals, many BDMs are available for free on numerous Internet sites. More detailed informa-tion usually has to be paid for, although some of the subscription sites may be free to access at an archive or library.

Monastery and convent records may also offer some information in punishment books, minutes of board meetings or letters to and from administrators, board members or trustees.

Poor laws and workhouses

The English Poor Laws, which provided poor relief in England and Wales, originated in the sixteenth century and underwent various amendments, such as the Elizabethan Poor Law (1601) and the Poor Law Amendment Act (1834). The laws were partially abolished in 1929, although some provisions remained in effect until the 1960s. The laws mandated that relief had to be provided by the parish in which a pauper was born. However, as industrialisation increased, so did the movement of people around the country. Poor Law Unions, often a combination of several parishes, were created to administer relief and were usually run by a board of guardians. These types of Unions were abolished in 1929.

The Poor Law system and its administration created a variety of records, such as meeting minute books, lists of inmates, health records and others. Poor Law records are particularly useful when looking for individuals who were discovered to be cross-dressing and cross-living.

There are numerous records of women who lived as men for years, sometimes their whole lives. When they fell on rough times, they had no choice but to enter a workhouse, where their biological sex was discovered. In addition, comments made by members of the boards of guardians can make interesting reading. In 1856 the *Illustrated Usk Observer* copied a Birmingham story about a 'A Female Confined in a Room for Fourteen Years.' The woman was described as 'one of those monstrosities of nature whose sex is doubtful' and the 'hair on her chin had grown to a considerable length'. She had been locked up in her family home for fourteen years. When discovered, she was removed to the workhouse. Although the story was widely circulated in newspapers at the time, no other information is available. Examining minute books, lists of inmates and health records may shed some light on what happened to her. Similarly, a 'General News' article in the *Birmingham Daily Post* reported that a man called Tom O'Brien, who was admitted to the Clogheen Workhouse in Tipperary in 1888, was found to be a biological female who had lived as a man for fifty years. There are many, many more similar stories.

Ancestry, which can be accessed for free at many archives and libraries, includes in its resources the *London, England, Workhouse Admission and Discharge Records, 1764–1930*. Keyword(s) searches in it are not effective, but names (real, not aliases) taken from newspaper reports can researched and lives fleshed out.

A useful website for advice on all aspects of workhouse records is Peter Higginbotham's *The Workhouse: The Story of an Institution* (2020). It includes useful links to archives holding Poor Law and workhouse records.

Health and death

Coroners' records

From the twelfth century onwards, coroners' held inquests into deaths that were violent, unnatural, of unknown cause or sudden (as well as treasure trove and shipwrecks). Not all coroners' records have been retained. Many were destroyed after a set number of years. Inquests may be covered in the press, and some records may be found by looking for cross-dressing and cross-living individuals. Most coroners' records are not available online, although a few themed collections exist. The Wigan and Leigh Archives Online have uploaded coroners' records from between 1917 and 1919 related to people killed in air raids during the war.[15]

Coroners' records often consist of several types of information:

- Coroners' day books
- Daily records kept to log the coroners' cases.
- Inquest files
- If an inquest was required to determine the cause of death, it took a form similar to court proceedings. Until 1926 inquests involved a jury, witnesses who were brought in to testify and the coroner, who provided the verdict. Inquests were often covered extensively in the press, particularly in sensational cases, such as murder. Files covering the proceedings can be vast and may include all evidence

presented, so they provide important information. My book, *The Veronal Mystery* (2020), was based on extensive files held by The Keep, the East Sussex Records Office at Brighton. After the death of Eric Trevanion in 1913, his 'close companion', Albert Roe, was suspected of being responsible. The inquest files show that homosexual evidence was suppressed, the public prosecutor failed to call vital witnesses and the coroner influenced the outcome.

- Coroners' inquests can be particularly useful for finding cross-living individuals, who would now be considered transmasculine. For example, John Coulter, a man who had been married for 23 years, died in a fatal accident in 1884. The inquest found John to be biologically female.
- Police reports
- Some coroners' inquest records may include police reports and witness statements. Others may not. The files on the case discussed in *The Veronal Mystery* had tantalising information revealed in the press and in the witness box. However, vital information from the police reports had not been retained.
- Post mortem reports
- Not all deaths require a post mortem report. When carried out they include a formal medical report on the condition of the body, both externally and internally. Examinations of men's anuses for homosexuality may be found in some post mortem reports. The 1913 autopsy card for Eric Trevanion held at the Wellcome Library, for example, contains the underlined words 'sexual pervert'.

Deaths

Death records are of limited use in locating LGBTQIA+ people, however, some do include additional information. For example, in a list of August–December 1802 burials in the Tarporley St Helen Parish records housed at the Cheshire Archives, the last entry reads 'a real hermaphrodite'.[16]

Health records

Health records include materials produced by doctors, hospitals and asylums. Those that are less than 100 years old will be closed under the Data Protection Act. If specific information is required, consult an archivist about possible access.

The National Archives, in association with the Wellcome Library, created an online *Hospital Records Database*, which identifies the existence of records from UK hospitals and directs researchers to the archives where they are kept.

Some records have not been used extensively in LGBTQIA+ studies and research, such as materials on the psychiatric treatment of women and bisexuals. Twentieth-century psychology primarily concerns men, particularly with reference to aversion therapies. Sarah Carr and Helen Spandler address the lack of evidence on lesbian and bisexual women who received treatment between the 1950s and the 1970s (Carr & Spandler 2019).

Earlier asylum evidence can be found. The story of Andrew Robertson is featured in 'Handlist 73 – Sources for LGBT (Lesbian, Gay, Bisexual, Transgender) History' produced by the Lancashire Archives. Robertson was admitted to Whittingham Asylum for having 'delusions' of 'belonging to the opposite sex' (Lancashire Archives 2011). Bristol Royal Infirmary archives have a file of 'drawings and prints of physical abnormalities and freaks' from 1735–1948, which includes a hermaphrodite.[17]

LGBTQIA+ men and women in the past might have been declared mentally ill or described as 'lunatics' or 'mad'. Local archives may hold hospital and asylum records related to such individuals. Anthony Rhys, who studies the outcast people of Wales, located the records of Kate Morgan, who was admitted to Glamorgan County Lunatic Asylum in 1902 after claiming she had been raped by a woman with whom she lived (Figure 8.1) (Rhys 2020).

Other pertinent records may include minutes of health trusts and local authorities, which track the provision of services.

Assorted archives

There is a great deal of material in archives, and the categories are too extensive to cover here. What follows are just a few suggestions.

Audiovisual

Audio

The last few decades have seen an increase in the number of oral histories of LGBTQIA+ people, particularly around anniversaries, such as the Wolfenden Report, when people realise that those alive during an event or period are aging. Oral history projects around civil partnerships and same-sex marriage have been carried out, and numerous local groups have sought to recover the memories of older people and their coming out stories. The Museum of Cardiff holds a collection of Welsh

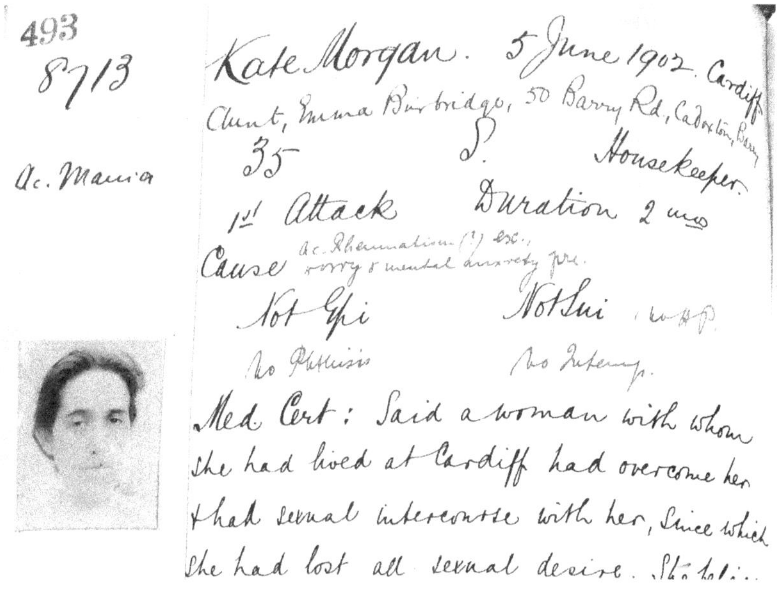
493
8713
Ac. Mania
Kate Morgan. 5 June 1902. Cardiff
Aunt, Emma Birbridge, 50 Barry Rd, Cadoxton, Barry
35 S. Housekeeper.
1st Attack Duration 2 mos
Cause Ac. Rheumatism (?) exc., worry & mental anxiety pre.
Not Epi Not Sui
No Phthisis No Intemp.
Med. Cert: Said a woman with whom she had lived at Cardiff had overcome her & had sexual intercourse with her, since which she had lost all sexual desire.

Figure 8.1 Glamorgan Archives DHGL/10/63 Case Notes for Angleton – Female Patients – 1864–1909.

LGBTQIA+ oral histories that I gathered.[18] Other collections and projects include the Hall-Carpenter Oral History Project at the British Library, Rainbow Jews, Brighton Ourstory, Our Story Liverpool, the Leicester LGBT Centre's Untold Stories project, among others. While some are available online, most are accessible upon request at the archive. Recordings may be covered under data protection laws, so access may be limited. The Oral History Society has a dedicated Lesbian, Gay, Bisexual, Transgender and Queer Special Interest Group, which notes on its webpage that 'many of these important collections … remain uncatalogued or held in places unknown to most researchers' (Oral History Society 2018). To address the issue, the group has an ongoing project to produce a map of LGBTQIA+ oral histories in the UK. While researching LGBTQIA+ oral histories is important, there is still the need to consider more general oral histories that include pertinent content. For example, a Liverpool Archives oral history from a 'Mr. Dalton' mentions in passing some homosexual sailors.[19]

Radio stations archive past programs, and it is worth searching their sites as well. A search of records from RTÉ, Ireland's national television and radio broadcaster, returned 820 hits for 'lesbian' and 933 for 'transgender'.

Podcasts are extremely popular, and they are produced by individuals and organisations of all kinds. *Gay Star News* published a list of '12 LGBTI Podcasts You Should Download and Listen to Right Now' (Wareham 2019). *Oprah Magazine* listed '12 LGBTQ Podcasts That'll Make You Proud Year-Round' (Donaldson 2019). Carrying out an Internet search for 'LGBT history podcasts' will produce a variety of lists and recommendations, such as *Bustle*'s '8 LGBTQ History Podcasts You'll Learn A Lot From'; 'Three Podcasts that Explore Queer History, Identity and Intimacy' from the *Washington Post* and many more (Thorp 2018; Carpenter 2017).

Some archives also produce podcasts and audio recordings on LGBTQIA+ history. A number of the recordings on the *Archives Media Player* on The National Archives website are tagged 'LGBT History'.

Visual

With so many film, tv, radio and streaming service companies in existence, there are many avenues for research into their dedicated materials. While many famous soaps and series have been analysed for LGBTQIA+ content and portrayals, little has been done on channels themselves. For example, the *History Channel* website has very poor returns for keyword(s) searches. Similarly, many channels split their content into categories. Searches for documentaries in these channels often provide few results. Some channels do run selections of films during LGBTQIA+ history or pride months. Rarely seen films can also sometimes appear.

There are numerous lists covering visual media. Various *Wikipedia* pages list 'LGBT-related films' and a number of subcategories, such as subject matter, characters, storyline or year made. Celebratory events, such as Pride, are often accompanied by articles and best film lists. *Rotten Tomatoes* has a list of '200 Best LGBTQ Movies of All Time' (2018). The British Film Institute (BFI), which runs the BFI Flare: London LGBTIQ+ Film Festival, published a list of the 'The 30 Best LGBTQ+ Films of All Time' (2018). The 'Search Moving Images' page on the *filmarchives online* website provides easy, free access to catalogue information in multiple languages from European film archives. Other lists and LGBTQIA+ content can be identified by searching for subjects like 'films/TV programmes with LGBT characters', 'animated films with LGBT characters', 'best LGBT movie/TV characters' or similar. Using these types of phrases and searching in books and journals will reveal analytical content on films and TV.

Searches in TV station archives may also produce results.

YouTube is another possible venue for research. Many individuals vlog about LGBTQIA+ history, and conferences often upload talks. For example, two videos from the 2015 'Researching within the LGBT Community' event at the University of Liverpool are available on *YouTube* and via the University of Liverpool website. Some cultural institutions have their own *YouTube* channels, such as Pride Cymru, which regularly uploads conference footage to its dedicated channel. Coming out vlogs are particularly popular on the platform, but searching for them can be problematic. Individuals often label and describe their content according to personal narratives, not necessarily in keyword(s) or searchable terms. As with book collections, users of *YouTube* can collate existing videos and become, in a sense, their own archivists. Collections can then be viewed either by what an individual collected or by themes. *YouTube* allows viewers to interact through a comments section, which can also be collected and studied. Inputting 'LGBTQIA+ research,' 'LGBTQIA+ history' or similar keyword(s) will identify a number of videos posted by individuals who engage in research or vlogging. Rowan Ellis and Dan Vo, for example, vlog extensively on queer history.

Community archives and community support groups

There have been a number of projects designed either to retain the records of local groups or generate material. Initiatives are often made possible through funding from grant bodies, such as the National Lottery Heritage Fund (NLHF, previously HLF) and Awards for All. Local group records can be found at a number of archives, such as Outreach Cumbria's collection from 1980–2016 at Carlisle Archives. It contains oral histories; leaflets, including some from the Campaign for Homosexual Equality (c.1983); books; newspapers; magazines and other items.[20] An HLF-funded project at Plymouth Museums Galleries Archives, Pride in Our Past, involved local LGBTQIA+ groups and individuals around the city collecting memorabilia, artefacts and, principally, oral history interviews. The project won the Community Archives and Heritage Group 'Most Inspirational' Community Archive award in 2011, although nothing seems to have been added since 2015.

More work needs to be done on black and minority-ethnic LGBTQIA+ groups and materials. A few projects do exist, such as the rukus! Black Lesbian Gay Bisexual Transgender Cultural Archive at the London Metropolitan Archives (LMA). Forty people, including volunteers, worked on the project. Among many achievements, they devised 891 catalogue descriptions. Projects like this, particularly those that consider other cultures, have the potential to expand the LGBTQIA+ list of keyword(s) and phrases.

Many of these types of projects result in exhibitions and publications. Often display boards or pop-up banners are retained by the local groups if heritage organisations do not have the facilities or space to retain such bulky items. For example, I curated four Welsh LGBTQIA+ exhibitions. The exhibition boards are in my garage, and I bring them out periodically to be put on view.

Divorce papers

Historically, homosexuality was cited in divorce proceedings. The publisher Emily Faithfull (1835–1895) was implicated in the 1864 divorce of Admiral Henry Codrington and his wife Helen. Throughout much of UK history, the church was responsible for granting divorces. In the eighteenth and nineteenth centuries, divorce was only accessible to the rich and required an Act of Parliament. It was slightly more accessible after 1857, when the courts were given the power to dissolve marriages in limited circumstances. Until the 1920s, all divorce suits were held in London. Divorce was expensive, thereby excluding poorer people. After the 1920s, the number of assize courts able to grant divorces was extended to ten. From the late 1960s, divorces were, and still are, heard at county courts.

Ancestry includes a *Divorce Case Files for England and Wales, 1858–1916* dataset from The National Archives, although it does not allow for keyword(s) searches. If names are found in newspapers, however, they can be searched and cross-referenced.

Personal papers

Letters and personal papers are worth checking for any indications of 'close companions' or similar terms. Some on broader themes can indicate attitudes of the day. An 1857 letter held at the Somerset Heritage Centre concerns a

> medical case involving a young lad of eleven years old and his belief that 'If boys are reared in a more effeminate way nowadays than the girls were 50 years ago, where is the surprise if they get girls' diseases and come home from the school hysterical'.[21]

Some letters will be closed under data protection regulations, but always talk with an archivist about possible access. Reproducing letters can have hidden difficulties. Copyright is an issue with the extensive correspondence between gay activists A. E. Dyson (1928–2002) and his partner Cliff Tucker (1912–1993), which is held at the University of Manchester John Rylands Library Special Collections. Copyright ownership was split between different charities, some of which no longer exist, making it extremely difficult to trace who now holds the rights.

Phone books

Phone books first started appearing in 1880, a year after public phones were first made available. BT Archives has a substantial historic collection of phone books, directories and telecommunications materials from throughout the UK that date back to 1846. They can be used for a variety of purposes.

While the national census is undertaken every ten years, phone books appeared almost annually, making it easier to track an individual's home or business. Phone books are also useful because the last published census is from 1911. The 1921 census will not be released until 2021. Widespread domestic use of the telephone did not become common until the second half of the twentieth century. Prior to that owning a phone was expensive, which gives an idea of an individual's economic status.

Edinburgh Befrienders (later Edinburgh Gay and Lesbian Switchboard) was founded in 1974, followed a day later by the launch of the well-known London Lesbian and Gay Switchboard. Other switchboards followed. Some were run by a single volunteer, such as the 24-hour gay helpline set up in Llandudno after a number of suicides in the area. In the two years before the helpline started at least five gay men killed themselves 'most of them young, ashamed and inexperienced. They have often been so unhappy that it is only after their deaths that their gayness came to light' ('Hell in Llandudno' 1976). Brian, the partner of one of the suicides, installed two telephones in his own home and at his own expense. Volunteers helped him provide 24-hour service.

Switchboards as well as LGBTQIA+ societies and groups can be traced through telephone listings. Telephone information in the 'Pink Press' also can be compared to mainstream phone books. Unfortunately, online searching in these types of resources is rarely possible. Part of the BT Archive is available through *Ancestry*, but keyword searching does not work because the surname field is mandatory and cannot be left blank. Appending words like 'switchboard' or 'society' alongside keyword(s) also does not work.

Local archives may house phonebooks and directories. However, because they consume an enormous amount of space, some institutions eliminate them from collections. Always check their availability with the archive or library before visiting.

Same-sex institutions

Same-sex institutions are those where participants, members or residents are restricted by sex: schools, military forces, prisons and borstals, convict or hulk ships, religious institutions and other similar organisations. Records in their archives may include references to 'sodomy', 'buggery' or similar terms. In punishment records, 'immoral' or 'unnatural' may appear.

'Handlist 73', the Lancashire Archives guide to researching LGBTQIA+ history, includes an entry from the Liverpool Juvenile Reformatory Punishment Book: 'Committing an act of indecency with another boy – 1 days cells' (Lancashire Archives 2011).

Some references can include a number of topics, leading to cross-referencing in other records. For example, letters from the Colonial Office held at The National Archives cover prisons and prison hulks. In June 1849 Charles Elliot, the governor of Bermuda, wrote to the Secretary of State complaining that incidents of 'unnatural crimes' amongst the convicts were 'apparently more prolific than the *Thames* hulk officers were aware of. Notes the men needed to move into a prison on shore as soon as possible.' The situation had not improved by October 1849 because Elliot wrote again about 'two convicts having been discovered in the act of "unnatural crime". He recommends that being severely whipped in private and kept in solitary confinement would be a better punishment than the publicity of a trial'.[22]

Modern records can include cases which reflect issues of the day, such as the age of consent. Somerset Archives holds the 1994–5 correspondence of Paddy Ashdown, MP, concerning 'the age of homosexual consent, the Criminal Justice and Public Order Bill and the case of Private Lee Clegg.'[23]

For the police, armed forces and similar bodies, searches can be carried out in punishment books.

Archival resources related to religious institutions may include the correspondence of religious people or church papers that reflect more generalised debates, such as discussions of sexuality and marriage held at Church of England General Synods.

Wills

Access to wills is generally only via physical archives. Little is available on the Internet. Where they are accessible, it is generally through subscription-based genealogical sites. Often only name searches are possible. The lack of keyword(s) search options for online wills and probate records is an issue. Hopefully, in the future, all searchable collections will allow generic keyword(s) searches by occupation, street address or other subjects, including LGBTQIA+ keyword(s) and terms.

Records from probate courts deal with the distribution of a person's estate after death. The 'Online Probate Indexes' page on The National Archives website is useful, although it has not been updated since 2012. It lists many county archives that include wills and probate records. It is useful to search for terms such as 'close companion', 'close friend' and other similar keyword(s). Often in same-sex relationships, partners willed their entire estates to each other, which often caused great controversy. In a dispute over the will of John Marsden, a letter from the 1830s in the archive discussed the 'unnatural practices' behind the two men's companionship.[24] Wills and probate files can also include gender diversity information, such as the 1630 will written by 'John Hobson Hermaphrodite.'[25]

Other archives

Many individuals own personal archives. I have assembled one of the largest collections of Welsh LGBTQIA+ material, and I know of other similar collections in private hands. Although some heritage organisations reach out to known collectors and individuals, people are often reluctant to place collections in archives during their lifetimes. It can mean having to travel to the archive to consult their own materials and, in some instances, having to apply for permission to consult their own collections. Individuals with extensive collections may want to talk to an archivist about preservation and suitable home storage, such as using acid free materials to prevent deterioration. Articles on conserving photos, documents, home archives and the like are available on the internet, but it is advisable to access advice from specialists in conservation, such as archives and museums.

Women's archives often include important LBT+ collections. The London School of Economics (LSE) Women's Library holds extensive materials, and its online search engine returns over a thousand hits for 'lesbian'. As usual, returns for 'bisexual' are much lower, with 250 hits. Various trans terminology returns varying hits. One of the stars of the collection is Vera 'Jack' Holme (1881–1969), a male impersonator who was very active in the suffragette movement and lived an active and fascinating life. There are letters to her partner, Evelina Haverfield (1867–1920), included in the collection. The LSE Women's Library regularly contributes to the collection of webpages uploaded to *UKWA* (UK Web Archive) to be kept for posterity.

The Glasgow Women's Library includes the Lesbian Archive, one of the most important in the UK. It is also one of the largest thanks to other archives donating collections. Its online search engine is limited. It returns only one hit for 'tribade', three for 'sapphic', three for 'intersex' and nothing for 'hermaphrodite'. The Library's 'LGBTQ Collections Online Resource' (2020) page includes a number of useful blogs, such as 'Early Lesbian and Gay Publications' and 'The Politics of Urania' by Niamh Carey. The page also offers a 'Bibliography' with useful links to other websites and podcasts.

Women's Archive Wales is a charity dedicated to preserving and promoting the records of women in the history of Wales. They collect records of women's lives and deposit them in an appropriate public repository. The materials can be accessed through the archives where they are held or through People's Collection Wales.

Other institutions have variants on women's archives, such as the Feminist Archive at Leeds University, Feminist Archive South at Bristol University and the Feminist Theory Archive at Brown University in Rhode Island. Still others have identified and collated information on their own collections, such as the 'Women in the Archives' initiative involving the Public Record Office of Northern Ireland and the Linen Hall Library or the 'Women in The National Archives' finding aid.

Some online archives

There are numerous online archives which can be explored. The only limit is that of determination. Just a few will be discussed here.

Searches using standard historic LGBTQIA+ keyword(s) in *Old Bailey Online: The Proceedings of the Old Bailey, London's Criminal Court, 1674 to 1913* produce limited returns. 'Hermaphrodite' returns two cases. In the first case, from 1719, a married woman, Katherine Jones, was charged with bigamy after she married Constantine Boone. Throughout the trial Jones claimed that Boone (referred to as 'it') was more woman than man, and, therefore, they could not marry. She was acquitted.[26] The second case involved a theft by Mary Tom House, identified as a spinster. A footnote explains that she was a hermaphrodite and had the Christian name of Tom.[27] A search for 'in male attire' returns the 1865 story of Sarah Geals, who married a woman.

Searches in the *London Lives 1690–1800: Crime, Poverty and Social Policy in the Metropolis* database using a number of historical, mainly male keyword(s) return results as well as information about the archives where original sources are located. *The Digital Panopticon: Tracing London Convicts in Britain & Australia, 1780–1925* facilitates searches in 50 datasets relating to the lives of 90,000 convicts sentenced by the Old Bailey. A search for 'sodomy' in it returns over 1,000 hits.

Using crime records from other countries' online archives can produce interesting results. A search for the term *sodomie* in *Gallica*, an extensive online library produced by the Bibliothèque nationale de France and dedicated to French written heritage, returns a list of offences from the Bastille.

Those involved in policing, public prosecutions or the courts may have archives, although many are covered by the Data Protection Act. Nonetheless, details may be requested under the Freedom of Information Act 2000, which allows anyone to request information held by public authorities, although the holding body can refuse to provide information if the request contains sensitive information or if it is too cost prohibitive.

A number of sites are now collecting and archiving websites from around the world, such as *Internet Archive* and *UKWA* (UK Web Archive). The latter project collects millions of websites every year. Not only can obsolete sites be recovered, but old versions of sites can be found and contrasted with changing views of organisations.

People's Collection Wales is an interactive site which provides a platform for individuals and organisations to upload information on Welsh history. The search term 'lesbian' returns 145 items. Most are from the LGBT+ collection at Glamorgan Archives, such as newsletters from The Older Lesbian Network (Wales). Other search terms are poorly served. However, a new project by the Museum of Cardiff in association with Pride Cymru is locating LGBTQIA+ material to upload to People's Collection Wales.

Materials from council and local government archives may be available on request, but some will be covered by the Data Protection Act. A useful way to check a council's commitment to local diversities is to check their equality plans, which may give insight into how local authorities interact with and view LGBTQIA+ people in their communities. Some councils simply copy and paste the Equality Act 2010, while others make an effort to include people with a broader narrative.

Other community-based projects may include dedicated content, such as *Historic England*, which is described as '400,000 of the most historically and architecturally significant places in England'. The description neglects to explain why *Historic England* also features places in Wales, Scotland and Ireland. The website includes 'Pride of Place: England's LGBTQ Heritage' (2020), which lists locations with a connection to LGBTQIA+ history, including sites in Wales (conforming to the persistent 'for Wales see England' meme).

The *John Johnson Collection* is an archive of eighteenth-, nineteenth- and twentieth-century printed ephemera from the UK produced through a partnership between the Bodleian Library and ProQuest. Various LGBTQIA+ search terms will produce results.

Dedicated LGBTQIA+ archives

Arguably, the first archive in the world on nonheterosexuality was the Institut für Sexualwissenchaft (Institute for Sexology), started in 1919 by German sexologist Magnus Hirschfeld in Berlin. The Nazi Party burnt it in 1933.

Internet searches for phrases along the lines of 'dedicated LGBTQIA+ archives' return a number of organisations – too many to list in full here. To search for dedicated archives in specific geographical areas, add Boolean commands, such as 'AND', to keyword(s) or phrases.

The *IHLIA LGBT Heritage* is an international archive and documentation centre in Amsterdam. It opened in 1999 after two significant collections were merged. It is one of the most significant and largest collections, particularly in relation to European material. It contains over 100,000 LGBTQIA+ books, journals, magazines, films, documentaries, photographs and objects. Other European archives include the Háttér Archive in Hungary, which started in 1997; Společnost Pro Queer Pamět (Center of Queer Memory) in Prague founded 2015; ŠKUC-LL in Slovenia, which contains The Lesbian Library and Archive established in 2001; and the *Queer* Archives Institute in Warsaw, which was founded in 2015. Of course, there are many more.

The ONE National Gay & Lesbian Archives at the USC Libraries in Los Angeles is a significant American collection established in 2010. It claims to be the largest repository in the world. Other North American archives include the Stonewall National Museum & Archives in Fort Lauderdale, FL, which started in 1984; the Lesbian Herstory Archives founded in the 1970s in New York; the Transgender Archives at the University of Victoria in British Columbia, which started in 2007; The ArQuives, founded in 1973, which primarily covers Canadian history and was previously called the Canadian Lesbian and Gay Archives; and the Pride Library at the University of Western Ontario. In 1978 the Australian Lesbian and Gay Archives opened, and it is still the only collection of its kind in the country.

In the UK LGBTQIA+ archives are plentiful. They include Brighton Ourstory, set up in 1989; the Cork LGBT Archive; the

Derbyshire LGBT+ Archive and the Plymouth LGBT Archive. The One Queer Gay Life archive in Cornwall, which began as The Sprocket Trust in 1995, can be found on the *LGBT History Cornwall UK* website. The National Library of Scotland aims to collect Scottish, UK and significant non-UK published material. The Lesbian Archive at Glasgow Women's Library is home to one of the most significant LGBTQIA+ historical collections in the UK. In Wales, Glamorgan Archives holds probably the largest collection of Welsh-related LGBTQIA+ historical materials.

Despite its name, the Lesbian and Gay Newsmedia Archive (LAGNA) at the Bishopsgate Institute in London holds material on all sexual orientations and gender identities. It houses over 200,000 press cuttings taken from the non-gay press as well as other publications and artefacts. The Bishopsgate Institute also hosts the archives of the pro-spective Queer Britain national LGBTQ+ museum. The Hall Carpenter Archives at the London School of Economics is a major resource for materials related to activism in the UK, particularly campaigning from the late 1950s to the 1990s.

In 2003 the London Metropolitan Archives (LMA) ran its first LGBTQ History and Archives Conference, now held annually, which recognises the importance of archiving personal and public collections. The LMA has several dedicated archives, including Speak Out London, an LGBTQIA+ oral-history community project, and rukus!, a Black lesbian, gay, bisexual and transgender (BLGBT) cultural archive. The LMA's LGBTQ History Club meets every month.

UK archives are often found in areas with sizeable LGBTQIA+ communities. As one would expect, in Manchester, home to the largest LGBTQIA+ population outside London, there are several archives, including those held at Central Library, the queerupnorth archive, OUT! Manchester and others. Brighton is another area in the UK with a large LGBTQIA+ population. The Keep, which includes the archives of the East Sussex Record Office (ESRO), holds a large collection and regularly publishes pertinent information on its website, including 'LGBT History Month: Coded Lives in the Archive – The National Lesbian and Gay Survey' by Jessica Scantlebury (2015).

Conclusion

In conversations with those involved in dedicated LGBTQIA+ archives, the message is clear. LGBTQIA+ history is being overlooked in mainstream archives and by the heterosexual and cisgender major-ity. While a number of archives have actively collected and promoted relevant material, they are in the minority. Information on sexual orientation and gender identity is poorly represented in digitisation initiatives. This may be due to the fact that certain archives do not have – or have not recognized – relevant content. Archival cataloguing is limited and may only record the collection name and a short description. While some do cite examples from criminal or health records, most only include catalogue descriptions rather than individual listings. However, those archives that have done so show that information can be tagged and uploaded as part of their equality work.

Certainly, some aspects of LGBTQIA+ history must be safeguarded as soon as possible. For example, the stories of those who lived at the time of the 1957 Wolfenden Report and when homosexuality was partially decriminalised in 1967 should be collected. These witnesses are aging, and their voices need to be recorded before they are lost.

Where information is shared by mainstream archives, it still tends to be dominated by male, and mainly criminal, narratives. Much work is still needed on women, trans and intersex. Also, research into less covered areas is needed, such as medical records and workhouses.

There is still a long way to go to record and archive the journey of LGBTQIA+ history.

Notes

1 The National Archives: Home Office and Prison Commission: Male Licences: PCOM 3/90/9406.
2 Rochester City Council Archives: RCA/J7/1/42.
3 Lancashire Courts of Quarter Sessions: Petitions: Kirkdale: Michaelmas 1875 QSP/3975/109.
4 Carlisle Archives: DWM – Waugh and Musgrave, Solicitors of Cockermouth: DWM/686/3.
5 Lancashire Courts of Quarter Sessions: Calendar of Prisoners: QJC/1a.
6 Lancashire Courts of Quarter Sessions: Calendar of Prisoners: QJC/1.
7 Lancashire Courts of Quarter Sessions: Indictment rolls: QJI/1/1753/Q3/54.
8 The National Archives: HO 144/30/73134.
9 'Sessions Held at Bodmin.' (1893). Kresen Kernow: Quarter Sessions: QS/1/21/212.
10 Quarter Session Records for the County of Somerset: Session Rolls for Epiphany 1746: Q/SR/314/172, Q/SR/314/159, Q/SR/314/170, Q/SR/314/171, Q/SR/314/173, Q/SR/314/165.
11 Buckinghamshire Archives: Records of the Court of Quarter Session: JC Justice Case Books: Q/JC/5/2.
12 Somerset Heritage Service; Taunton, Somerset, England; *Somerset Parish Records, 1538–1914*; Reference Number: D/P/twn/2/1/3.
13 Gloucestershire Archives: Marriage and Blessing of Mark Read and Sigurd Vandendriessche: Reference number D11526/1.

14 Glamorgan Archives: D1227 Casgliad Norena Shopland Collection: Same-sex Consultation D1227/16.
15 Wigan Coroner's Court, Register of Inquests, 1917–1919. Wigan Council. Accessed online at https://archives.wigan.gov.uk/archive/court-records/cor oners-court/register-inquests
16 Cheshire Record Office: P22 – Tarporley St Helen Parish: Combined Registers: P 22/1/6.
17 Bristol Archives: Bristol Royal Infirmary 1735–1980: Richard Smith Papers 1735–1948: 35893/36/r.
18 Museum of Cardiff: Oral Histories, LGBT Excellence Centre, 2020, OE1313.
19 Liverpool Archives: North West Sound Archive: (LIVSA Box 31): 382 DOC/135.
20 Carlisle Archives: DSO 148 OutReach Cumbria 1980–2016: DSO 418.
21 Somerset Heritage Centre: Papers of the Dickinson Family of Kingweston: DD/DN/4/4/133.
22 The National Archives: Records of the Colonial Office: CO 37/127/24; CO 37/128/20.
23 Somerset Heritage Centre: Papers of the Rt. Hon. Paddy Ashdown MP: Legal: Miscellaneous. 1994–1995: A/BHI/1/27/7.
24 Lancashire Archives Handlist 73 – RCHY/5/1/56.
25 Lancashire Archives Handlist 73 – WCW/K 1630 John Hobson.
26 Old Bailey Proceedings Online (www.oldbaileyonline.org version 8.0, 18 December 2019), September 1719, trial of Katherine Jones, alias Nowland (t17190903-50).
27 Old Bailey Proceedings Online (www.oldbaileyonline.org version 8.0, 18 December 2019), September 1719, trial of Mary Tom House (t17670909-24).

Bibliography

'200 Best LGBTQ Movies of All Time.' (2018). *Rotten Tomatoes: Rainbow Tomatoes – Your LGBTQ Viewing Guide*. Accessed online at https://editoria l.rottentomatoes.com/guide/best-lgbt-movies-of-all-time

'A Female Confined in a Room for Fourteen Years.' (1856). *Illustrated Usk Observer*. 19 April. p. 4.

Brunow, Dagmar. (2020). 'Naming, Shaming, Framing?: The Ambivalence of Queer Visibility in Audio-visual Archives.' In Anu Koivunen, Katariina Kyrölä & Ingrid Ryberg (Eds.). *The Power of Vulnerability: Mobilising Affect in Feminist, Queer and Anti-racist Media Cultures*. Manchester: Manchester University Press. pp. 175–194. doi:10.7765/9781526133113.00017.

Burke, Jason. (2018). 'Tanzania: Men Arrested for "Gay Marriage" Face Anal Examinations.' *The Guardian*. 8 November. Accessed online at https://www.theguardian.com/world/2018/nov/08/tanzania-men-arrested-for-gay-marria ge-face-anal-examinations

Carpenter, Julia, (2017). 'Three Podcasts that Explore Queer History, Identity and Intimacy.' *The Washington Post*. 12 June. Accessed online at https://

www.washingtonpost.com/news/soloish/wp/2017/06/12/three-podcasts-tha
t-explore-queer-history-identity-and-intimacy

Carr, Sarah & Spandler, Helen. (2019). 'Hidden from History?: A Brief
Modern History of the Psychiatric "Treatment" of Lesbian and Bisexual
Women in England.' *The Lancet*, vol. 6, no. 4. pp. 289–290. doi:10.1016/
S2215-0366(19)30059-8.

Donaldson, Zoe. (2019). '12 LGBTQ Podcasts That'll Make You Proud Year-
Round.' *The Oprah Magazine*. 21 August. Accessed online at https://www.
oprahmag.com/entertainment/g28764034/best-lgbt-podcasts

'General News.' (1888). *Birmingham Daily Post*. 5 March. p. 8.

'Hell in Llandudno.' (1976). *GW* (unknown publication).

Higginbotham, Peter. (2020). *The Workhouse: The Story of an Institution*.
Accessed online at http://www.workhouses.org.uk

Lancashire Archives. (2011). 'Handlist 73 – Sources for LGBT (Lesbian, Gay,
Bisexual, Transgender) History.' *Lancashire County Council*. Accessed
online at https://www.lancashire.gov.uk/media/52095/Handlist73-LGBT.pdf

'Lesbian, Gay Bisexual and Trans (LGBT) History.' (2020). *South West Heritage Trust: Somerset Archive Catalogue*. Accessed online at https://som
erset-cat.swheritage.org.uk/researchGuides/lgbt

'LGBT History.' (2020). *The National Archives: Archives Media Player*.
Accessed online at https://media.nationalarchives.gov.uk/index.php/tag/
lgbt-history

'LGBTQ Collections Online Resource.' (2020). *Glasgow Women's Library*.
Accessed online at https://womenslibrary.org.uk/explore-the-library-and-a
rchive/lgbtq-collections-online-resource

Morris, Charles E., III & Nakayama, Thomas K. (Eds.). (2014). 'GLBTQ
Pasts, Worldmaking Presence' [Special Issue]. *QED: A Journal in GLBTQ
Worldmaking*, vol. 1, no. 2.

National Archives, The. (2012). 'Online Probate Indexes.' *The National
Archives: Your Archives*. Accessed online at https://webarchive.nationala
rchives.gov.uk/+/http://yourarchives.nationalarchives.gov.uk/index.php?title=
Online_Probate_Indexes

National Archives, The. (2020). 'How to Look for Records of Sexuality
and Gender Identity History.' *The National Archives*. Accessed online at http
s://www.nationalarchives.gov.uk/help-with-your-research/research-guides/ga
y-lesbian-history

Oral History Society. (2018). 'LGBTQ: Lesbian, Gay, Bisexual, Transgender
and Queer Special Interest Group.' *Oral History Society*. Accessed online at
https://www.ohs.org.uk/about/introducing-special-interest-groups/lgbtq

'Out Lit – Our LGBT Collections.' (2020). *Surrey County Council*. Accessed
online at https://www.surreycc.gov.uk/libraries/borrow-or-renew/collections-
and-reading-lists/out-lit-our-lgbt-virtual-collection

Peterson, Trudy Huskamp. (2013). 'HRWG Newsletter: News of March 2013.'
International Council on Archives. 9 April. Accessed online at https://www.
ica.org/sites/default/files/HRWG_2013-02_newsletter_EN_0.pdf

'Pride of Place: England's LGBTQ Heritage.' (2020). *Historic England.* Accessed online at https://historicengland.org.uk/research/inclusive-heritage/lgbtq-heritage-project

'Researching within the LGBT Community.' (2015). *University of Liverpool: engage@liverpool.* Accessed online at https://www.liverpool.ac.uk/engage/events/2015-2016-programme/researching-lgbt-community

'Resources About Archives.' (2020). *JISC: Archives Hub.* Accessed online at https://archiveshub.jisc.ac.uk/guides/resourcesaboutarchives

Rhys, Anthony. (2020). Email message to author. 5 February.

Scantlebury, Jessica. (2015). 'LGBT History Month: Coded Lives in the Archive – The National Lesbian and Gay Survey.' *The Keep.* 18 February. Accessed online at https://www.thekeep.info/lgbt-history-month-coded-lives-archive-national-lesbian-gay-survey

Schmidt, Laura. (2016). 'Using Archives: A Guide to Effective Research.' *Society of American Archivists.* 26 March. Accessed online at https://www2.archivists.org/usingarchives

'Search Moving Images.' (2020). *filmarchives online: Finding Moving Images in European Collections.* Accessed online at http://www.filmarchives-online.eu/searchmask

Shopland, Norena. (2020). *The Veronal Mystery.* Cardiff: Wordcatcher Publishing.

Shopland, Norena & Leeworthy, Daryl. (2018). *Queering Glamorgan: A Research Guide to Sources for the Study of LGBT History.* Glamorgan Archives. Accessed online at https://glamarchives.gov.uk/wp-content/uploads/2018/08/Queering-Glamorgan-28Aug2018.pdf

'The 30 Best LGBTQ+ Films of All Time.' (2018). *BFI.* 19 July. Accessed online at https://www.bfi.org.uk/news-opinion/news-bfi/features/30-best-lgbt-films-all-time

'The Extraordinary Male Impersonation Case.' (1884). *Belfast News-Letter.* 22 January. p. 3.

Thorp, J. R. (2018). '8 LGBTQ History Podcasts You'll Learn A Lot From.' *Bustle.* 7 October. Accessed online at https://www.bustle.com/p/8-lgbtq-history-podcasts-youll-learn-a-lot-from-12104540

Wareham, Jamie. (2019). '12 LGBTI Podcasts You Should Download and Listen to Right Now.' *Gay Star News.* 3 May. Accessed online at https://www.gaystarnews.com/article/gay-queer-lgbti-podcasts-digital-pride

Zepeda, Lizeth. (2018). 'Queering the Archive: Transforming the Archival Process.' *disClosure: A Journal of Social Theory,* vol. 27, article 17. doi:10.13023/disclosure.27.14.

9 Researching in museums

Britain is blessed with a wide variety of museums. As of 2020, *Museums. co.uk*, a web directory of independent UK museums, lists 1,722 cultural institutions. *Historic UK: The History and Heritage Accommodation Guide* provides a useful map of museums in England, Scotland and Wales colour coded by type, such as maritime, general or local (Johnson 2020).

Reports from various heritage or tourism associations have shown a consistent rise in museum visitor figures, particularly in the last ten to fifteen years as museums moved away from being object-based and inward looking toward being more audience-based and outward looking. The 2019 annual report of the UK's Department for Digital, Culture, Media and Sport (DCMS) on their sponsored museums shows 49.8 million visits for 2018/19, an increase of 48 percent since records began in 2003. Most of the DCMS museums are large, city-based national or specialist museums, however, with the British Museum returning the largest number of visitors.

Another DCMS 2019 survey, 'Taking Part', interviewed roughly 10,000 individuals in England for the same period and showed that 50.2 percent of respondents had visited museums and galleries in the previous twelve months. The survey included reasons for visiting. The most popular motivation was a 'general interest in the subject of the museum/collection'. Barriers for not visiting museums were, firstly, the lack of time and, secondly, a lack of interest. There are no comparable studies from Wales, Scotland or Northern Ireland.

'Taking Part' showed that 27.6 percent of respondents used a heritage website or app. Of those who used digital tools, 44.4 percent wanted to learn about heritage or the heritage environment. However, for LGBTQIA+ people wishing to learn of their heritage, most British museums have little on offer.

Some small, rural or specialist museums may have only one page on a council website or a limited dedicated site. Those with more extensive sites that include searchable collections invariably return no hits for LGBTQIA+ keywords, leaving national museums or those in cities or large towns the only options for performing keyword(s) searches. This does not mean these smaller or more specialist organisations do not have content. The materials may not be included online. However, even nationals can produce poor search results. The British Museum produces a reasonable number of returns from online searches of their collections, however 'transgender' is poorly represented with only three hits. National Museums Scotland searches return a small number of hits, as do online searches in the National Museum of Wales. Searches of the National Museum of Northern Ireland site, however, produce no returns.

Given that the first port of call for most museums and archives is their online collections, if LGBTQIA+ material is not included or is poorly displayed, then the overriding impression is that the organisation does not care to engage with LGBTQIA+. Care needs to be taken over tagging, and it is important that museums upload at least some details to show a duty of care toward a portion of society traditionally overlooked.

In the past few decades, both the definition and purpose of museums have changed as they become more outward looking. More institutions are engaging with communities by marking celebratory calendar events, such as Black History Month, or notable anniversaries, such as the end of WWI. As a result, some changes in LGBTQIA+ representation have taken place, particularly among the large museums. It still remains true, however, that very few museums, not just in the UK but worldwide, have permanent representation of LGBTQIA+ people. This lack of representation means LGBTQIA+ people are not present in what is supposed to represent a shared history.

Some small, local museums are run by long-serving boards of trustees dominated by white, middle-class, well-educated males who promote heterosexuality and binary gender as the unwritten norm. Efforts to advance and include diversity can be denied or blocked. However, many others are supportive, although LGBTQIA+ representation in museums is typically temporary and largely coincides with either annual celebratory periods, such as Pride or LGBT+ History Month, or notable anniversaries, such as the 60th anniversary of the Wolfenden Report (2017), the 50th anniversary of partial decriminalisation of male homosexuality in the UK (2017) or the 30th anniversary of Section 28 (2018). Frequently these activities are driven by local LGBTQIA+ communities or self-identified/allied staff, and projects are funded by community grants.

The difficulty with temporary or pop-up exhibitions tied to celebratory dates is that they set aside LGBTQIA+ content from the mainstream by confining it to a limited period. An added problem is that host museums rarely retain exhibition panels or pop-up banners. Instead, they remain the property of the community group. Because organisations may have shifting volunteers and often have limited storage space, panels and banners may be disposed of or lost. Conversely, pop-up museums and exhibits can be beneficial, particularly when held off-site, if they involve those who traditionally do not visit museums due to the lack of representation.

LGBTQIA+ tours are popular temporary events held at some museums. These walks around museums or cultural sites are usually led by volunteers who have been trained by an LGBTQIA+ historian.

One of the earliest was done in 2014 at London's V&A. According to Dan Vo (2015), 'queer performer Bird la Bird gave a one-off whistle-stop tour called "Swoosh Around the V&A". With megaphone in hand, she rambunctiously rechristened the V&A the People's Queer Knick-Knack Emporium.' A year later the V&A's LGBTQ Working Group arranged the first of many tours, which are now so popular they are run weekly. The V&A also provides a downloadable booklet entitled 'Out on Display' by Dawn Hoskin (2014), a useful 'LGBTQ Terminology' guide to aid with searches and an 'Out in the Museum' blog (2020).

In 2018 the British Museum launched a self-led LGBTQ trail entitled *Desire, Love, Identity: LGBTQ Histories*. It now consists of two trails complete with downloadable audio commentaries. The first, a 15-object trail, takes around 90 minutes and includes the famous Warren Cup. The second, three-object trail takes half an hour to complete. The trails are complimented by a 2013 book by R. B. Parkinson entitled *A Little Gay History: Desire and Diversity Across the World*, which details 40 items from the British Museum's collection.

Other museums have followed suit. The University of Cambridge Museums and Botanic Garden, which has nine cultural sites, runs 'Bridging Binaries' LGBTQ+ tours across seven of their museums (and include gay penguins). The Museum of London runs a monthly 'Queer City: The Museum of London LGBTQ+ Tour. In 2020 Amgueddfa Cymru – National Museum Wales launched its first tour. Other institutions with tours include the Tate and Oxford University Museums. It is advisable to check museums' websites to see if they offer LGBTQIA+ tours or provide links to other options, such as local walking trips, which are certainly growing in popularity.

As I wrote in 'Queering the Welsh Museum' (2020), queer tours need to offer more than the same roundup of international characters, such as Roman emperors and famous artists. They must try to be more locally based. Welsh, Scottish and Irish tours should focus more on national subjects, which may provide opportunities to run two tours and increase visitors. All staff at heritage organisations also need to be proficient in LGBTQIA+ terminology and possible relevance in order to recognise content which has been either missed or deliberately supressed.

What is in the museum

One of the difficulties in finding out what exists in museum collections is that an item may not be catalogued or tagged as being of LGBTQIA + interest, either because its significance was not known or it was deliberately obscured. A number of museums have been reassessing their collections in an effort to move away from traditional meanings and interpretations, which can include an overreliance on Western or imperial interpretations and the prevalence of male, white and class-dominated terminology.

When reassessing collections, it is necessary to be alert for possible LGBTQIA+ material, and those doing the assessing must be proficient in LGBTQIA+ terminology and attuned to possible relevance. If unsure, content should still be tagged, nonetheless, possibly with an added question mark. Researchers and others with more knowledge can decide on the merits of an item's inclusion in LGBTQIA+ history. Consultation is important.

At the 2013 London Metropolitan Archives *LGBTQ History and Archives Conference*, Clare Barlow, an assistant curator at the National Portrait Gallery, spoke about the dilemma of choosing appropriate pronouns for text panels accompanying a 1792 portrait of Chevalier d'Eon (1728–1810), which was acquired by the Gallery in 2012 (Barlow 2013). Despite d'Eon's lifelong campaign to live as a woman, curators chose to use 'he' for consistency, both in describing d'Eon on the text panels and in the context of wider Gallery communications. The Gallery's decision was challenged at the conference, and Sean Curran claimed that it had 'decided *not* to open up a dialogue about the challenges of choosing an appropriate pronoun' (Curran 2013; Curran 2019, p. 137). The Gallery did address criticism about the choice, however, and now the webpage about the portrait avoids pronouns.

Traditional meanings and terminology promoting heteronormative and binary gender narratives need to be challenged. Double standards also need to be addressed. Proof of heterosexuality is rarely required when confronted with material related to an opposite-sex couple. Yet, when same-sex couples are considered, there is usually the rider of not being able to prove they had sexual relations – as if sex proves sexuality. The criteria for differentiating between romantic friendships and same-sex relationships outlined in Chapter 4 should be considered, which allows researchers the opportunity to make their own interpretations or pursue further research. Promoting those items which can be questioned will engage a wide range of people interested in LGBTQIA+ history.

Queering museums

As visitor figures have risen over the last ten years, there has also been a rise in people writing on 'queering museums'. An internet search along those lines will return numerous papers, blogs, submission requests and other materials on alternative media, such as *YouTube* videos, *Soundcloud* audio streams and podcasts.

Two of the dominant themes of these discussions are how to queer museums and how to queer objects.

A number of museums have been examining their collections for queer readings. In 2015 the National Museums Liverpool launched a project to identify LGBTQIA+ objects and created a dedicated 'LGBT+ Collections' (2020) page on their website. Similarly, the V&A and the British Museum examined a number of their collections. Reactions to these efforts can be notable. After R. B. Parkinson's *A Little Gay History* (2013), which details 40 objects in the British Museum, was published, someone posted on *Twitter*: 'When will the Met do this?' (Parkinson 2016, p. 41). Searches in The Met's online collection do return hits for some LGBTQIA+ keyword(s). Another response discussed by Parkinson was an incident in the British Museum's bookshop concerning an elderly man who broke down on the phone when ordering a copy. The man

> explained his tears by saying that he had been imprisoned when a teenager for being gay, that while he was in prison his lover had killed himself, and that he wept because he had never expected to find a national institution including his history. That – not any official strategy – is why institutions have to publish such books. Our history is past, present and personal.
>
> (Parkinson 2016, pp. 41–2)

The incident happened just six years before this book was written, so it is clear that LGBTQIA+ history still has a long way to go.

As well as reinterpreting existing collections, museums are concentrating on the vital work of collecting new material. The process of collecting is not always straightforward.

Section 28, brought into British law in 1988, had a damaging effect on public bodies. This piece of legislation banned any local authority from 'promoting' homosexuality. As schools, museums, archives and the like received funding from local authorities, they were included in the ban. It was a completely ineffective piece of legislation. There was not a single prosecution, despite blatant contraventions. I was involved in two LGBTQIA+ exhibitions before the Act was repealed in 2003, one with LAGNA and the other with the Museum of London. However, Section 28 gave organisations an excuse to either not collect or not raise awareness of items by tagging or identifying them as LGBTQIA+. Opportunities were lost to create and preserve a history. Many collections from the late twentieth century were thrown away. Many times have I been told that people carted boxes of photos, letters and documents around from garage to garage or loft to loft until they either grew tired of moving everything or the items became mouldy and were thrown out. Much has been lost.

Organisations will often promote their interest in collecting material during celebratory calendar events or through pop-up exhibitions. Much of this material is political, such as badges or t-shirts. More personal accounts come less from object-based collections and more from oral histories and stories. However, much of what museums do collect goes into the archival stores, only to be brought out again for occasional inclusion in temporary exhibitions or events.

Mainstream inclusion does not necessarily have to include physical materials. A change in interpretation is possible through descriptive labels on permanent displays. Alterations in exhibit language can prevent any assumptions on the part of the visitor, challenge existing perceptions of heteronormativity and binary genders, disrupt the silence that surrounds sexuality and gender diversity in museum displays and allow possible layers of interpretation for visitors to consider.

Given that most 'queering museums' activities have been carried out by large museums holding international collections, the results reflect the institutions' heritage of collecting. Many of the objects are from Roman and Greek times or colonial countries. Strip away the international elements, and what are we left with? At national museums, which represent a nation's people, what is on offer for LGBTQIA+ people?

LGBTQIA+ materials and content in museums varies enormously and is heavily dependent on being tagged as such. It is worth searching a museum's website before visiting to see what has been included or identified. Some have very comprehensive coverage, such as the Museum of London, which lists LGBTQIA+ collections that include printed matter and artefacts relating to a whole range of topics, such as health awareness, religion, civil rights, eighteenth- and nineteenth-century satirical drawings, Oscar Wilde and the theatre, and the Suffragette movement (Collinson 2019). The Museum also has recordings of interviews with LGBTQIA+ activists. A number of objects from the collection are presented online. Other institutions have more modest offerings. The collection of the Herbert Art Gallery and Museum in Coventry, for example, includes *Other Wise*, a monthly magazine for gay and lesbian people that was distributed in the Coventry area in 1988.

Similar to the British Museum's Private Case collection of obscene print materials, which was transferred to the British Library in 1973, some museums had 'obscene' closets or rooms which could be viewed only by appointment and usually only by men. The *Gabinetto Segreto* (Secret Cabinet or Secret Museum) of the Museo Archeologico Nazionale di Napoli is a collection of erotic art now on permanent display. The British Museum's *Secretum* was created in 1865 to house objects and artefacts deemed obscene. The objects were subsequently removed and dispersed to more relevant collections. It is worth asking if a museum has a Secret Cabinet.

Queering museums, by necessity, does include queering certain objects either because they have clear indicators of same-sex activity, like the Warren Cup, or they are interpreted as having a queer aspect. This in itself raises numerous questions. Can a piece be considered queer if the creator was, or was perceived to be, LGBTQIA+? Does a picture of a cat by Gwen John (1876–1939) qualify as 'queer'? By drawing attention to the creator, are we detracting from the piece? If labels should include an indication that a creator was queer, then, in the interest of equality, should other labels indicate a creator was heterosexual or unknown?

Objects can be used as pointers. For example, in 2018 the Science Museum included a Spitfire in their 'Queering the Science Museum' tour to talk about Roberta Cowell, the first British trans woman, simply because she flew Spitfires during WWII. Feedback for the tour revealed that over 50 percent of respondents had not visited the Science Museum within the past year (Armstrong 2019).

Some objects can have wider community connections. As David Shariatmadari (2019) points out:

> The plaster reproduction of Michelangelo's David in the [V&A] museum's cast room satisfies all of these [V&A object selection]

requirements, by virtue of the homoerotic friendship between bib-lical figures David and Jonathan, Michelangelo's reputed homo-sexuality, and the fact that the statue was used as a discreet come-on by travellers returning from the grand tour. 'If you brought back a statue of David and had it on your shelf, it was usually an invitation, a hint for others to approach you and say, I think there might be things we can talk about.'

Historic houses

Coded objects like souvenir David statues can be seen in venues other than museums, such as historic houses, which often have high visitor numbers. The DCMS 2019 'Taking Part' household survey in England reported that 72.4 percent of respondents had visited a heritage site. Indeed, the house itself can be queered. In 2017 the National Trust explored LGBTQIA+ history at their sites to coincide with the 50th anniversary of the partial decriminalisation of homosexuality in 1967. The aim was to discover how LGBTQIA+ people shaped properties cared for by the Trust. A page dedicated to the initiative, 'Prejudice and Pride: Exploring LGBTQ History' (2020), is accessible on the National Trust website. Historic England also has a webpage, 'Pride of Place: England's LGBTQ Heritage' (2020), which includes a user con-tributed, interactive map of locations significant to LGBTQIA+ his-tory and heritage.

Some properties are visitor magnets. Anne Lister's home Shibden Hall in Halifax became popular following 'Gentleman Jack,' the TV series about her life. Sissinghurst Castle, the Kent home of the bisexual author Vita Sackville-West and a place where radical les-bian groups used to meet in the 1860s and 1870s, attracts a number of visitors. Plas Newydd in Llangollen has attracted the famous and the ordinary interested in viewing the house of the Ladies of Llangollen.

The impact of these places can be assessed by reading tourist's comments. Jane Hoy and Helen Sandler included visitor comments in their *Living Histories Cymru* play on the Ladies of Llangollen, which was performed in several locations in Wales, including Plas Newydd (Hoy 2018).

Other non-historic venues, such as pubs, bars and clubs, have dis-appeared over the years, often leaving nothing behind but a few ads or photos. Aware of this gap in collecting LGBTQIA+ history, the Museum of Cardiff rescued as much as they could when a popular gay bar, the King's Cross, shut down in 2011.

Should there be a queer museum?

Most countries in the world do not have dedicated LGBTQIA+ museums, despite the fact that many dedicated individuals and groups are trying to establish them. However, some organisations that define themselves as archives do hold collections of artefacts, so the boundaries are blurred.

The Schwules Museum in Berlin became the first dedicated LGBTQIA+ museum when it opened in 1985. It is now the world's largest and most significant LGBTQIA+ museum. The second dedicated museum was the GLBT Historical Society in San Francisco, which in 2010 expanded into the GLBT Historical Society Museum. Other institutions offer more specialised collections. Art is the focus of New York's Leslie-Lohman Museum (formerly the Leslie-Lohman Museum of Gay and Lesbian Art). The National Gay and Lesbian Sports Hall of Fame was established in Chicago in 2013. The World AIDS Museum, formed in 2013, is in Fort Lauderdale, Florida.

Wikipedia includes an 'LGBT Museums and Archives' category, but it is not comprehensive.

Despite previous abortive attempts by others, there is an initiative to set up the first dedicated museum in the UK, Queer Britain, which aims to open in 2021. Its website includes a number of 'Virtually Queer: Queer Britain's Digital Archive' oral history project videos. The Unstraight Museum of Sweden is currently digital only, but they have a long-term goal of developing a physical museum.

Despite existing and intended dedicated museums, the question is often asked, Should there be queer museums? To which the answer is, Should there be black, Jewish, Gypsy/Roma/Traveller and other identity museums?

Conclusion

Reports from the Department for Digital, Culture, Media and Sport show that visitor figures, at least for some museums in the UK, are increasing. Audience growth may be due in part to museums taking a more outward looking, rather than object-based, approach to exhibitions and collections, which is reflected, for example, in visitor feedback from the Science Museum's queer tour.

However, generally, LGBTQIA+ people are not well represented in museums, either in online collection searches or in permanent collections. As long as they are not included, the overriding impression is that organisations and cultural institutions do not care to engage with LGBTQIA+ people or their history.

Bibliography

Armstrong, Eleanor. (2019). 'Queering the Science Museum.' *Viewpoint: Magazine of the British Society for the History of Science*, no. 119. June. pp. 4–6. Accessed online at https://www.bshs.org.uk/wp-content/uploads/Viewpoint_119_web_v3.pdf

Barlow, Clare. (2013). 'Soldier, Spy, Celebrity Transvestite?' *National Portrait Gallery Blog*. 20 February. Accessed online at https://www.npg.org.uk/blog/soldier-spy-celebrity-transvestite

'Bridging Binaries: LGBTQ+ Tours at Cambridge Museums.' (2020). *University of Cambridge Museums & Botanic Gardens*. Accessed online at http s://museums.cam.ac.uk/bridgingbinaries

'Bridging Binaries: LGBTQ+ Tours at the Polar Museum.' (2019). *Cambridge Live Tickets*. Accessed online at https://www.cambridgelive.org.uk/tickets/events/bridging-binaries-lgbtq-tours-polar-museum

Collinson, Alwyn. (2019). 'Hidden Pride: London's LGBT History.' *Museum of London*. 2 February. Accessed online at https://www.museumoflondon.org.uk/discover/london-pride-london-lgbt-history-gay-rights

Curran, Sean. (2013). '"Unspeakable" LMA LGBTQ History and Archives Conference.' *Towards Queer Blog*. 11 December. Accessed online at http://towardsqueer.blogspot.com/2013

Curran, Sean. (2019). 'Queer Activism Begins at Home: Situating LGBTQ Voices in National Trust Historic Houses.' Doctoral Thesis. UCL (University College London). Accessed online at https://discovery.ucl.ac.uk/id/eprint/10072804

Department for Digital, Culture, Media and Sport (DCMS). (2019). 'DCMS-Sponsored Museums and Galleries Annual Performance Indicators 2018/19.' *GOV.UK*. Accessed online at https://www.gov.uk/government/statistics/sponsored-museums-and-galleries-annual-performance-indicators-201819

Department for Digital, Culture, Media and Sport (DCMS). (2019). 'Taking Part Survey: England Adult Report, 2018/19.' *GOV.UK*. Accessed online at https://assets.publishing.service.gov.uk/government/uploads/system/uploads/attachment_data/file/879725/Taking_Part_Survey_Adult_Report_2018_19.pdf

Hoskin, Dawn. (2014). 'Out on Display.' *V&A Blog*. 3 September. Accessed online at https://www.vam.ac.uk/blog/news/out-on-display

Hoy, Jane. (2018). 'Writing Festival Theatre: Living Histories Cymru.' *Lesbian Gay Bisexual Trans + History Month*. 23 October. Accessed online at https://lgbtplushistorymonth.co.uk/2018/10/jane-hoy-helen-sandler-writing-festival-theatre

Johnson, Ben. (2020). 'Museums in England, Scotland and Wales.' *Historic UK: The History and Heritage Accommodation Guide*.' Accessed online at https://www.historic-uk.com/HistoryMagazine/DestinationsUK/Museums

'LGBT Tours of National Museum Cardiff Aim to Reveal Secrets.' (2020). *BBC News*. 15 March. Accessed online at https://www.bbc.co.uk/news/uk-wales-51839437

'LGBT+ Collections.' (2020). *National Museums Liverpool.* Accessed online at https://www.liverpoolmuseums.org.uk/collections/lgbt-collections

'LGBTQ Terminology.' (2020). *V&A: LGBTQ Working Group.* Accessed online at https://vanda-production-assets.s3.amazonaws.com/2017/01/26/11/55/20/6673a913-a8dd-4b04-a649-6026f5f2f440/LGBTQ%20terminology.pdf

'LGBTQ+ History Month.' (2020). *Museum of London.* Accessed online at https://www.museumoflondon.org.uk/museum-london/whats-on/exhibitions/lgbt-history-month?series=LGBTQ%20month

'Out in the Museum' [Blog] (2020). *V&A: LGBTQ Working Group.* Accessed online at https://www.vam.ac.uk/info/lgbtq#out-in-the-museum

Parkinson, R. B. (2013). *A Little Gay History: Desire and Diversity Across the World.* London: The British Museum Press.

Parkinson, R. B. (2016). 'A Little Gay History, from Ancient Egypt to the Modern Museum: A Personal View.' In *Queering the Collections.* pp. 21–46. Amsterdam: IHLIA, Reinwardt Academie en de auteurs. Accessed online at http://comcol.mini.icom.museum/wp-content/uploads/sites/9/2019/01/Queering_the_Collections_publicatie_light.pdf

'Prejudice and Pride: Exploring LGBTQ History.' (2020). *National Trust.* Accessed online at https://www.nationaltrust.org.uk/features/prejudice-and-pride-exploring-lgbtq-history

'Pride of Place: England's LGBTQ Heritage.' (2020). *Historic England.* Accessed online at https://historicengland.org.uk/research/inclusive-heritage/lgbtq-heritage-project

Shariatmadari, David. (2019). '"Shout Queer!" The Museums Bringing LGBT Artefacts Out of the Closet.' *The Guardian.* 8 July. Accessed online at https://www.theguardian.com/culture/2019/jul/08/queer-museums-pride-lgbtq-tour-pitt-rivers-v-and-a

Shopland, Norena. (2020). 'Queering the Welsh Museum.' *Wales Arts Review.* 22 April. Accessed online at https://www.walesartsreview.org/visual-arts-queering-the-welsh-museum

Steorn, Patrik. (2012). 'Curating Queer Heritage: Queer Knowledge and Museum Practice.' *Curator: The Museum Journal,* vol. 55, no. 3. pp. 355–365.

'The Chevalier d'Eon.' (2020). *National Portrait Gallery.* Accessed online at https://www.npg.org.uk/research/new-research-on-the-collection/the-chevalier-deon.php

'Virtually Queer: Queer Britain's Digital Archive.' (2020). *Queer Britain.* Accessed online at https://queerbritain.org.uk/virtually-queer

Vo, Dan. (2015). 'Why the V&A Gay and Lesbian Tour is Essential.' *V&A Blog.* 23 April. Accessed online at https://www.vam.ac.uk/blog/museum-life/why-the-va-gay-and-lesbian-tour-is-essential

Conclusion

The suggestions put forward in this book for avenues of research are not exhaustive. They are intended to illustrate some of the tools that can be used to explore LGBTQIA+ areas and subjects.

Language is one of the most important tools a researcher can use. There is no definitive LGBTQIA+ dictionary in book form. While numerous glossaries and dictionaries exist online, in almost all there are omissions, particularly of archaic terms. Arguably, what is needed is more data from the deep past, rather than what is covered by modern terminology. Sexologists writing of sexual matters in the late nineteenth century often used Latin to keep such knowledge from the masses. Similarly, journalists and writers would often obscure their meaning through euphemism or idiosyncratic language, making the exact nature of their discussions murky. Many existing glossaries do not work when researching historical subjects and time periods, and a much wider range of keyword(s) is needed to uncover information, which was the motivation behind the *Queering Glamorgan* (2018) 'pick-and-mix' glossary. Hopefully, other word and vocabulary lists, such as IHLIA's *Homosaurus*, will be expanded to include terms from this book and *Queering Glamorgan*. Familiarity with terminology enables readers and researchers to recognise content, even when not specifically looking for it. It should be noted, however, that this book reflects my personal research areas and interests, mainly women and transmasculine and Welsh. Work still needs to be done on transfeminine and intersex to expand those keywords and phrases.

Once armed with a more extensive vocabulary, research can be expanded significantly, particularly when using online digitised platforms, such as newspaper databases. Public writers are more likely to mix up and separate out terminology. By studying these kinds of writings, LGBTQIA+ glossaries can be expanded and forgotten or unpublished stories can be recovered.

The search for information can take the researcher into interesting areas, such as genealogy. The identification of LGBTQIA+ people is let down in genealogical tools, however, by the domination of names and the absence of searchable themes. For example, wills should be searchable by keyword(s), such as 'close companion' or similar. Moving away from the dominance of name searching will open up genealogy sites to more extensive research by historians of numerous subjects, not just those working on LGBTQIA+ history. One way to address this issue would be to allow users to universally tag items, thereby providing researchers quick access to specific types of data. Having a queer genealogy would be useful for other areas of research, such as locations associated with LGBTQIA+ history. For example, Emily Skidmore (2017) shows in *True Sex* that transmen were more likely to live to rural areas.

Tagging is being used more frequently on the myriad websites that regularly upload hundreds of books, journals and other digitised texts and images. However, LGBTQIA+ history suffers from a discrimination of disinterest, and more people uploading or tagging items for others to find is needed. This also applies to libraries, archives and museums. More information needs to be tagged, and more information needs to be uploaded to cultural institutions' online sites. The 'search our collections' web page is a portal. If organisations want to attract people to their premises to simply visit or carry out further research, they need to demonstrate a commitment and show that they consider LGBTQIA+ history an important subject. At the moment this is not happening in most libraries, archives and museums. These organisations also need to break away from a reliance on celebratory days and months. They must begin to consider permanent representation. If they claim to represent the people of a nation or a local area, as many do, how can they argue for or continue such exclusion? While this situation persists, there will always be a need for stand-alone repositories where local material may be sent, although they may thereby deprive particular localities of more diverse collections in county archives and museums.

There is a well-used phrase, 'Nothing about us without us'. All organisations which host LGBTQIA+ events must consult and include LGBTQIA+ people. We, in turn, must try to recover as much information as possible and place it in the public domain, because only then will society accept that sexual and gender diversity is a part of normal life.

Hopefully, this work assists in that recovery.

Bibliography

IHLIA LGBT Heritage. (n.d.). *Homosaurus: An International LGBTQ Linked Data Vocabulary.* Accessed online at https://homosaurus.org

Shopland, Norena & Leeworthy, Daryl. (2018). *Queering Glamorgan: A Research Guide to Sources for the Study of LGBT History.* Glamorgan Archives. https://glamarchives.gov.uk/wp-content/uploads/2018/08/Queering-Glamorgan-28Aug2018.pdf

Skidmore, Emily. (2017). *True Sex: The Lives of Transmen at the Turn of the Twentieth Century.* New York: New York University Press. pp. 43–67. doi:10.2307/j.ctt1pwt5nm.

Index

For Product Safety Concerns and Information please contact our EU
representative GPSR@taylorandfrancis.com
Taylor & Francis Verlag GmbH, Kaufingerstraße 24, 80331 München, Germany

www.ingramcontent.com/pod-product-compliance
Lightning Source LLC
Chambersburg PA
CBHW050526270326
41926CB00015B/3096

9 780367 564582